# Improving Quality and Performance in Your Non-Profit Organization

by Gary M. Grobman

White Hat Communications
Harrisburg, Pennsylvania

Published by White Hat Communications.



The material in Chapter 4 of this publication is from the *Benchmarking Workbook for Nonprofit Organizations*, a work-in-progress by Jason A. Saul. Copyright 1998 Jason A. Saul. This chapter is part of a larger work by the author to be released by the Wilder Publishing Center, St. Paul, Minnesota, in 1999. Used with permission. For more information on this book and other Wilder Foundation publications, call 1-800-274-6024, or visit their Web site at www.wilder.org.

The quotation from John Nash from the *National Productivity Review* which appears on page 109 is copyrighted material (1993) and is reprinted with permission from John Wiley and Sons, Inc.

The material which comprises Appendix B is from *Out of Crisis*, ©1986 by the W. Edwards Deming Institute, published by the Massachusetts Institute of Technology, Center for Advanced Educational Services, Cambridge, Massachusetts, and is reprinted with permission.

The material which comprises Appendix C is copyrighted material provided by Reginald Carter, supplemented by material prepared by Frederick Richmond and Eleanor Hunnemann, and is reprinted with permission.

Contact the author in care of White Hat Communications, or by e-mail at: *gary.grobman@paonline.com*

Printed in the United States of America.

Proofreading: Barbara Trainin Blank
Editing: Linda Grobman, John Hope
Library of Congress Catalog Card Number: 98-96842
ISBN 0-9653653-4-4

# Table of Contents

# FOREWORD

It is about time that a knowledgeable executive sat down and examined the effect of quality management on the not-for-profit industry. I was delighted to learn that Gary Grobman had done just that and even more pleased when he asked that I write a foreword to the book. He has done a meticulous job of research and has given the matter a lot of thought.

My first exposure to the need for managing quality came when I entered industry at the bottom of an organization. The overwhelming operating concept was that the laws of nature and probability were against any process working correctly. The thought was that variation overwhelmed everything, which is kind of like thinking the sun revolves around the earth. No one thought about the need for quality anywhere other than manufacturing in this regard. I felt that was incorrect and over many years in the workplace, including 14 as vice president of ITT, I developed the ideas and practices of prevention that led to several books and the founding of Philip Crosby Associates in 1979 to teach management and employees about getting things done right the first time.

The first clients of PCA were manufacturing companies who were having problems with foreign competition concerning automobiles, copiers, electronics and such. After a while we began to see insurance, hospitality, and administrative organizations coming to the Quality College. All of them had the same problems; they just had different words for doing things wrong. We had to learn those words in order to help them understand that quality was not goodness, that it was conforming to the agreed requirements; that it came as a result of preventative efforts, not from a system; that the performance standard was Zero Defects, not acceptable levels of quality; and that nonconformance was measured in financial terms, not by indexes. We then helped the management teach everyone else, gave them some tools to work with, and watched them reduce waste and errors dramatically. Most dropped from 25% of revenues to below 5% in a short time. Quality Improvement comes about quickly when management quits making problems for itself.

I was on the Board of Trustees for a hospital and for a college during those years. Whenever I mentioned to those in management that they could benefit from finding a common philosophy of quality the response was that they were not profit-oriented. They felt they were different. Actually they were exactly the same, they just had different words for managing money, like "retained earnings," rather than "profit." The thought that people in "for-profit" companies are motivated by the company making money is really not valid. Very few people in the organization understand where money comes from and how to count it. Employees and suppliers are both turned on by the reliability of the organization, not by its cash flow.

Management's job is to create this reliable organization, and that is what quality management is all about. Most everyone makes it much more complicated than it really is, and turns it into a system of procedures. Actually it is a philosophy of managing that concentrates on having an agenda everyone can understand; requirements that meet the needs of employees, suppliers, and customers; building successful relationships; and having a worldly outlook.

It was the lack of a worldly outlook that kept non-profit organizations from coming to the Quality College at first. Many senior people had the idea that quality was for factories where everything was straightforward. Yet hospitals are factories where many processes are conducted regularly each day and where people work together to make products. A heart bypass operation is a product. In educational institutions, there is a planned transfer of knowledge as well as the managing of facilities and personnel.

Once non-profit managers began to realize this, they took the teachings of our Quality College to heart and caused dramatic changes in their organizations, some of whom are talked about in the text.

We must always be looking for ways to understand our work better so we can become more useful and reliable as organizations and as individuals. Gary's book will help.

Philip Crosby
Winter Park, FL

# Preface

I never had more than a minimal exposure to issues relating to quality improvement during my 13 years as the CEO of a non-profit organization, nor much more while authoring several books on non-profit management. In researching this book, I have come to understand that I was not alone in my ignorance about these issues within our sector. Like most who run non-profit organizations, my primary focus was a host of survival issues—how to secure enough funds to meet payroll, how to get vital work done when a sick employee is absent, how to communicate information to a key board member who asked for it today and wanted it yesterday, and how to accomplish the mission of the organization despite an indomitable tidal wave of paperwork.

My introduction to TQM came as a result of an assignment in a Master's level "Research Methods" class at Penn State University, a course I was taking in preparation for entering a Ph.D. program in Public Administration. Everyone in the class was asked to read and summarize an article on TQM. To this day, I haven't figured out what this assignment had to do with the course, which was designed to teach us how to use statistical methods to conduct scientifically valid research. It was not until the following semester, when I was enrolled in a Ph.D. seminar entitled "Research and Theory in Public Management," that I became inundated with references to TQM, not only in the textbooks and other reading material, but also by the in-class comments of my classmates.

For my term paper in this Public Management class, I chose the topic "Total Quality Management in the Healthcare Industry—Fad or New Paradigm?" I immersed myself in the TQM literature and found a lot that I believe has value to non-profit executives concerned with improving the quality and performance of their organizations.

Frankly, I became fascinated with what TQM has to offer, and at the same time bewildered by the massive failure of this management philosophy to penetrate much of the non-profit sector, except for the healthcare industry. After reviewing hundreds of articles about TQM, I found very few that related to the non-profit sector other than hospitals, and precious few books.

In making inquiries to academicians and practitioners about my search for readable and practical TQM literature, I was greeted with an ambivalence about the desirability and validity of TQM interventions. Some of those responses steered me in other directions related to change management. TQM is passé, but check out Theory of Constraints, one professor affiliated with Penn State recommended. Another from Seton Hall University attested that BPR was the current rage, and another sent me to the burgeoning stacks of books touting outcome-based management, an innovative tool of choice for many non-profits. A personal friend who is a consultant to non-profit organizations told me of his experiences with Large Group Intervention. When I read a book on the relevance of chaos theory to public management, bells went off in my head saying that this might well be the aspect of management theory that explains how organizations begin, evolve, and react to change.

What do the management techniques I write about have to offer non-profit managers? What I have done with this book is to provide a taste of change management techniques in a non-profit context, in a readable, practical format. There are lots of books on each of these techniques, but I haven't found any that provide an introduction to more than one in the same book, and certainly none is available that is geared to an audience of non-profit managers and board members.

Experience has shown that many principles of management are generic in that it does not matter if they are applied to organizations in the private sector, public sector, or voluntary sector. Many of the best minds in management theory do not make a distinction in the type of organization for which their advice applies, and thinkers such as Herbert Simon, Peter Drucker, and Phil Crosby have provided classical principles of management that are interdisciplinary. For many readers, this will be their first exposure to formal change management strategies such as TQM, BPR, benchmarking, LGI, and OBM. I've tried to explain these strategies in a way that is not too threatening, if not actively inviting.

An additional purpose of this book is to provide easy access to additional resources on the Internet. I have included Web sites that are informative, free, and, presumably, will be continually updated not only with information about the change management strategies in this book but about entirely new ones that evolve.

## Purpose of This Book

The purpose of this book is to present a case for non-profit organizational leaders to continually assess the quality and performance of their organizations' programs, and to take steps to continually improve that quality and performance. Quality improvement may sound like an amorphous concept, and this book seeks to provide the framework for non-profit leaders to take concrete actions to improve quality, not just talk about it.

## Who Should Use This book

This book should be of benefit to non-profit executives who are looking for ways to keep their organizations as competitive as they can be. Non-profit organization board members should also find this book useful. In their governance, they need to be asking questions about quality that, in today's environment, are rarely being asked at board meetings. This book can also be used as a textbook in non-profit management classes. There is an expansion of academic programs geared toward practicing and future non-profit executives.

## What This Book Does

In Chapter 1, I discuss why quality improvement is an important, but often neglected, aspect of non-profit management as we are entering the 21st century.

In Chapter 2, I write about Total Quality Management (TQM) and why this change management strategy has taken center stage as the change management strategy of choice for thousands of organizations.

Chapter 3 provides an introduction to Business Process Reengineering (BPR), which many see as a logical successor to TQM in facilitating dramatic, radical improvement in organizations.

Chapter 4, written by Jason Saul, is an introduction to benchmarking and best practices, the process of systematically identifying and adapting other organizations' successful ideas to improve one's own performance. I am grateful that Mr. Saul, a national expert on benchmarking as applied to non-profit organizations, agreed to share his expertise with readers of this book.

Chapter 5 introduces outcome-based management as a technique to judge whether an organization is truly accomplishing what it sets out to do rather than merely providing services, regardless of the value these services add to the lives of clients. This chapter was co-authored by Frederick Richmond.

Chapter 6 is an introduction to Large Group Intervention techniques, and was co-authored by Gerald Gorelick, an organizational development consultant now in private practice.

Chapter 7 provides an introduction to chaos theory. This theory seeks to explain what happens in dynamic, non-linear systems in both nature and in organizations, and offers insights into obtaining dramatic changes in organizational performance.

In Chapter 8, I discuss the role of non-profit organization boards in improving quality of their organizations. Boards are increasingly evolving beyond the honorary governing bodies they once were, and must be full partners with management for improving quality and performance in organizations.

My concluding comments are included in Chapter 9. In this chapter, I describe some of the leading theories of organization, and discuss the limitations of a scientific approach to managing organizations.

At the end of each chapter, there is an interview with a non-profit organization leader, consultant, or association executive, in which you will read about some personal experiences with a change management intervention technique.

TQM teaches that one should adopt a philosophy of continuous improvement. White Hat Communications intends to publish subsequent editions of this book, and it is my intention to take the TQM philosophy to heart and improve each succeeding edition. Your comments and criticisms about this book would be appreciated as I begin to revise it to make it more valuable to my "customers."

This is my fourth book published by White Hat Communications of interest to non-profit organizations. Prior books have been *The Pennsylvania Non-Profit Handbook*, now in its fourth edition; *The Non-Profit Handbook, National Edition*, which is based on the Pennsylvania handbook; and *The Non-Profit Internet Handbook*, which was co-authored by Gary Grant, Associate Dean for External Affairs of the University of Chicago's School of Social Service Administration. I look forward to continuing my collaboration with this forward-looking publishing company, and I am grateful to the company's founder and owner, my wife, Linda, for her support and encouragement in completing this manuscript.

**Acknowledgments**

The author gratefully acknowledges Dr. Christopher McKenna and Dr. Jeremy Plant, both on the faculty of the School of Public Policy at Penn State University (Harrisburg). Dr. McKenna was responsible for introducing the concept of TQM to me in his "Research Methods" class, and Dr. Plant made numerous suggestions for improving the draft of my paper that was submitted in his "Research and Theory in Public Management" class and were incorporated into Chapter 2 of this book.

Thanks also go out to the consultants, non-profit executives, and association executives who gave me their time to be interviewed for this book. Their insights added to what you are reading in the sidebars in which their interviews appear, and they also pointed out books, articles, and other resources to me. I was delighted when Philip Crosby, one of the patriarchs of quality management, agreed to write the Foreword for this book. His writing on quality issues has been an inspiration to me, and his influence in this field is legendary.

Thanks also are due to the proofreaders and editors, including Linda Grobman and John Hope, and those who read all or parts of the manuscript and suggested improvements, including Dr. Lawrence Martin, Dr. John McNutt, Dr. Ann Whitney Breihan, and Michael A. Sand. I wish to thank Jason Saul, the author of Chapter 4, *Introduction to Benchmarking*, for his contribution to this book, and to Gerald Gorelick and Frederick Richmond for coauthoring chapters with me. Finally, I wish to thank my family for allowing me the opportunity to finish this book. I promise to wait a few months before beginning my next one.

*Gary M. Grobman*

# 1
# Introduction to Quality Improvement

Many of those who govern and manage non-profit organizations are increasingly finding their organizations subject to many of the same economic pressures as their for-profit counterparts. Their operations often resemble their for-profit competitors in both organizational structure and corporate culture. They are increasingly led by those trained in business rather than social work, and their mentality and style of administration often reflects this. Stereotypically, they often put the "bottom line" paramount above the needs of clients. One non-profit CEO I spoke with recognized the inconsistency of trying to run a human service organization and retaining his "humaneness," while at the same time being forced to make rational business decisions, which meant the firing of "nice" people who were hurting the performance of his organization. He commented to me that his management credo was to be "ruthlessly altruistic."

In many cases, the products and services once provided solely by non-profit, charitable organizations are now being provided by for-profits. One can often find health clubs, hospitals, schools, nursing homes, and day care centers—both for-profit and non-profit—competing for clients on an equal basis within communities. When there is this direct competition, particularly in the delivery of human and educational services, cost is just one factor in a customer's decision. Quality of service is often even more important in a decision, and those non-profits that offer high-quality products and services obviously have a competitive edge. Those that can't offer quality may find themselves out of business.

Many thousands of other non-profit organizations find themselves in a situation where they don't have direct economic competition from those providing the same service. There is only one United Way affiliate in each community, one Arts Council, one Arthritis Foundation, one AARP affiliate, and one Special Olympics affiliate. Except under unusual circumstances, it is unlikely that another organization will sprout up to directly challenge one of these. It would be easy to jump to the conclusion that having a monopoly of this nature would mean that quality and performance are not as important as they are to those with direct, head-to-head competition for providing a particular product or service.

Nothing can be further from the truth. Quality is important to all non-profit organizations, and none is immune from the consequences of neglecting quality. Charities rely on loyal customer support. Even if a non-profit is not involved in direct economic competition, there is substantial competition for things that indirectly affect the viability of organizations. Among them are—

1. **Competition for government and foundation grants.** Most charitable non-profits depend on grants to supplement any client fees they receive. Foundations are acutely aware of organizations with poor reputations with respect to skimping on service quality. No one wants to be associated with such an organization. It is no wonder that first-class organizations often have little trouble attracting funding, because everyone wants to be associated with them.

2. **Competition for private donations**. Would you make a donation to a charity that had a reputation of treating its clients like animals? Unless that organization is the SPCA, you are more likely to look elsewhere for finding a charity worthy of your donation.

3. **Competition for board members.** Why would anyone want to serve on a board of a second-class non-profit and risk being condemned or otherwise embarrassed by the media, the political hierarchy, and clients? There are only so many skilled, committed civic leaders in each community who are willing to donate their time and expertise to serve on non-profit boards, and it is clearly not attractive to serve on the board of a charity with a reputation for having poor quality.

4. **Competition for volunteers.** What can be said for board members goes double for service delivery and other volunteers. No one wants to be associated with an organization with a reputation for poor quality. Many volunteers see their volunteer work as a springboard for a career, and volunteering for a pariah in the community does not serve their interests.

5. **Competition for media.** The media play an important role in helping a non-profit charity promote its fundraising, encourage clients to utilize its services, and improve employee morale. Poor quality can result in the media ignoring an organization or, worse, highlighting its shortcomings for the entire world to see.

6. **Competition for legislative and other political support.** Non-profit charities have benefited from the support of political leaders, directly through the provision of government grants, and indirectly through the provision of favors such as cutting government red tape and legislation solving the problems of the agency and those of its clients. Political leaders are certainly not going to be responsive to an organization if they receive letters of complaint about the organization's poor quality.

7. **Competition for qualified employees.** Particularly during the current climate of low unemployment, quality non-profits find that they have less employee turnover and find it easier to attract employees to fill vacancies and for expansion.

The consequences of having poor quality, or the reputation (public perception) of having poor quality, can result in the board of directors throwing up its hands and deciding to liquidate the organization. Or, in extreme cases, having the government step in and liquidate the organization. Imagine the aftermath of a child care agency that failed to perform a quality background check on an employee who later was found to be a child abuser. Or the hospital that failed to adequately verify that a staff member it hired was adequately board-certified.

As pointed out by Dr. John McNutt of Boston College's Graduate School of Social Work, most, if not all, states look at the community benefit provided by a non-profit organization in considering whether it is eligible for non-profit status in the first place. Quality and community benefit are inextricably linked.

In 1998, a scandal affected international agencies that raise funds for child welfare. Who knows how many millions of dollars will not be contributed to these agencies because some agency official did not feel it was important to inform donor sponsors that their sponsored child had died several years ago?

With a public already conditioned as a result of the 1992 United Way of America scandal and the 1995 New Era Foundation scandal to be wary about charities, non-profits need to be more vigilant about not only quality issues affecting the delivery of direct service, but about those that affect fiscal accountability as well.

The cost of quality, or the lack thereof, often exceeds what is perceived to be saved by neglecting quality. Read the newspapers and you can find many examples of the consequences of poor quality in non-profit organizations. Owners of personal care boarding homes have failed to see the value of installing sprinkler systems and, as a result, have seen the loss of life and of their properties. Doctors have mistakenly removed the wrong kidney from a patient. Hospital maternity ward staff have given the wrong newborn to the wrong parents. The ramifications far exceed the financial loss and loss of prestige to the organization—human suffering for the clients and potentially huge, successful lawsuits against the non-profit organization as a result of a preventable lapse in quality-related policies.

For the typical non-profit that doesn't deliver client services, quality should mean much more than the ability to answer the telephone on the first ring. It means having a newsletter without typographical errors. It means having an attractive, periodically updated Web site. It means spelling the names of donors correctly in substantiation letters. It means delivering on promises made to legislators for follow-up materials. It means having conferences where participants feel that they get their money's worth. It means assuring that each board member has the information necessary and appropriate to make governing decisions. It means that volunteers know in advance what is expected of them.

And for those that deliver direct human services, it means, among other things—

- treating each client with the dignity he or she deserves
- respecting confidentiality
- providing on-time services
- providing resolution to legitimate complaints
- providing services in a safe and secure setting
- providing services in a facility that is accessible, clean and functional
- delivering services provided by competent, trained personnel

- assuring that services provided meet high standards and respond to the clients' needs
- obtaining informed consent from clients before services are provided
- seeking constant feedback from clients to improve the delivery of services
- taking advantage of advances in technology to improve communication between the organization and its clients.

The quest for quality improvement in organizations has been the subject of intense research. Every few years or so, a potentially transformational way of improving management outcomes—either in government or business and industry—is touted in academic journals, professional publications, and, eventually, in the popular press. Total Quality Management (TQM), Planning and Program Budgeting System (PPBS), Zero-Based Budgeting (ZBB), Management By Objectives (MBO), and, more recently, Business Process Reengineering (BPR), and Large Group Intervention (LGI), have been, or are becoming, mantras for improving organizational performance. Each is accompanied with its own statistical and software tools, lingo, culture, and hype. With each new program, a myriad of organizational consultants appear from nowhere, each hawking expertise and promising Nirvana —selling workshops, workbooks and computer software, and definitely improving *their own* organizational outcomes, if not those of their deep-pocketed clients.

For many reasons that may not be completely known without further empirical research, some of these new concepts once extolled and ballyhooed as chemistry eventually become stale and are relegated to alchemy. Managers who once swore by these techniques come to swear at them. Perhaps each technique was grounded in valid theory, but when implemented over time, serious unintended consequences developed that could not be foreseen by their creators.

One such potentially revolutionary way of managing organizations, Total Quality Management (TQM), swept through private U.S. business organizations in the 1970s and 1980s, and was being adopted in some form by thousands of government organizations and non-profit organizations, principally those that are healthcare-related, in the 1990s. Chapter 2 provides an introduction to TQM.

## Up Close—Joe Geiger

"Quality improvement is critical to an organization's credibility. It takes energy and commitment and resources but the payback warrants the investment," asserts Joe Geiger. He is in a position to know. Geiger is on the front lines of defending the interests of the non-profit sector, having served as the executive director of the Pennsylvania Association of Non-Profit Organizations (PANO) since 1995.

The purpose of PANO is to monitor the opportunities and threats to the charitable non-profit sector in Pennsylvania arising through government. The organization provides coalition-building leadership to address such issues and serves as a resource to elected officials. PANO also provides technical assistance and education to Pennsylvania's charitable non-profit community as well as develops and promotes useful publications and educational workshops.

As the principal spokesperson for charitable interests in Pennsylvania, Geiger has weathered the storms created by non-profit scandals at the state and national levels (the now-defunct New Era Foundation was headquartered in Radnor, Pennsylvania), and he believes that the sector is primed for changes in how it views its role in society. He has witnessed firsthand the quality improvement revolution, and thinks that non-profits have a lot to learn from their for-profit counterparts.

"The non-profit sector has been less attuned overall to quality issues than the for-profit sector, although there are some shining examples of very sophisticated non-profit organizations," he points out. "Generally, many non-profit organizations lack the skills, vision, and resources to get involved in formal change management interventions. Some do quality improvement instinctively. Some are more formal in the approach as witnessed through agendas for board retreats and ongoing training. But it is hard to do formal training when you are driven by organizational survival issues (as most are)," he laments.

Geiger maintains that quality issues are important largely because non-profit organizations need efficiency, they need to treat people correctly, and they have to be accountable to their funding streams.

"Funders do not want their names attached to shabby work," he says. "All people possess a dignity and should be treated as such, and sloppy work can exhaust limited resources more rapidly and completely than high-quality work."

According to Geiger, PANO has engaged in an ongoing effort for quality.

"We are motivated to stand as a role model for Pennsylvania," he says with pride. "The PANO Board and staff hold quality as a high value and want to be perceived as such. High quality is imperative for PANO to attract the funding necessary to flourish and attract additional members."

One manifestation of PANO's drive for quality is its quarterly surveys in its newsletter, *Keynotes.* "We always attach 5-10 questions so our members have an easy forum to let us know what they are thinking and needing," he says. "We do an annual phone survey of all of our members to explore customer satisfaction and complete missing information for our database. We send out feelers to collect opinions on public policy issues, what types of speakers members want for the annual conference, and other miscellaneous requests."

The organization staff also participates in formal training to improve its business processes and to assure that PANO membership needs remain its principal focus. PANO conducts weekly staff meetings with ongoing computer software training and program training. An organizational consultant comes in monthly to assist staff with projects. The consultant reviews what staff is doing and assesses how it is consistent with retreat goals. The same consultant facilitates the annual board and staff retreat.

Geiger asserts that quality improvement should be high on the agenda of every non-profit organization.

"Any organization not doing quality improvement will not survive the scrutiny, funding challenges, and competition with for-profit businesses into the next millennium," he relates. "It can take less time to do something correctly the first time versus going back to fix a mistake. It also gives an opportunity to fix inevitable mistakes. We are often more critically evaluated on how we repair a problem or mistake than how we operate through routine periods," he points out. The PANO Board is fairly active in tracking issues involving the quality of PANO programs and activities, Geiger says.

"It is challenging to have a lot of involvement when you are a statewide organization in a state the size of Pennsylvania. The annual retreat has gone a long way in making sure the board plays a healthy role in the quality of services we deliver," reports Geiger. "The evolution of functioning standing committees is expanding the volunteer role in attaching quality to what we do. I believe the attention paid to hiring an executive director with a strong experiential background has also made a difference. The resulting hiring of quality staff ensures quality in operations and programming."

Despite the obvious benefits to the organization of running quality programs, resistance to change still comes about. "Sometimes resistance will come from staff when they get into overload," Geiger says. "However, we found that the break in routine to keep never-ending improvement on the radar screen helps staff continue to be highly functional."

# 2
# Introduction to Total Quality Management

It doesn't seem to matter whether the organization manufactures microchips or potato chips. Or whether it manufactures service for eight or delivers services itself. It claims to offer something valuable to the world's largest, most sophisticated businesses as well as to your pre-teen's lemonade stand. It is touted as working equally well, albeit with a few adjustments, in for-profit organizations and non-profit organizations. This management philosophy is sweeping through government at all levels as well—bringing transformational change to management practices of organizations as diverse as the Department of Defense and municipal governments of one-horse towns.

Total Quality Management, or TQM, has, in recent years, been acclaimed as the road to organizations capturing the Holy Grail, or at least the Baldrige Award or its comparable accolade for non-profit organizations, the Excellence in Service Quality Award. It may even have something to offer individuals in managing their private lives as well, but this has yet to be explored to any great extent.

While TQM has yet to solve the intractable problems of curing AIDS, bringing about world peace, ending world hunger, or eliminating the busy signal of America Online, its adherents assert it is only a matter of time before it successfully manages to ameliorate virtually any intractable problem—if only those organizations working on these problems would implement TQM as intended. Its detractors—and they are legion—generally criticize TQM on the difficulties of implementing it rather than the principles themselves.

TQM has had a colossal sway on business management in the last two decades. If it were just another management fad, it would be difficult to explain why the "market penetration" of TQM not only has increased within sectors, but has been adopted by new sectors, such as the healthcare industry.

The term "total quality management" has overshadowed virtually all aspects of management programs for almost three decades now in the United States with an aura of apparent invincibility. Like the term "managed care," its meaning is not particularly precise, perhaps an indication more of its changing contextual framework to adjust to conditions rather than a reflection of amorphous content. It has come to mean a philosophy as much as a management technique or tool.

A concise definition appears in an article by Karen Bemowski in the February 1992 issue of *Quality Progress*:

> *TQM is a management approach to long-term success through customer satisfaction...based on the participation of all members of an organization in improving processes, products, services, and the culture they work in.*

"In discussing TQM with health and human service agencies, I have found it necessary to differentiate it from 'quality assurance (QA),'" says Dr. Lawrence Martin of Columbia University. "Quality assurance is after the fact and evaluates a service's compliance with professionally derived standards. TQM is up front (let's build quality in at the beginning) and is derived not from professionals but from consumers."

TQM is a general approach to management that seeks to improve quality, reduce costs, and increase customer satisfaction by restructuring traditional management practices. It requires a continuous and systematic approach to gathering, evaluating, and acting on data about what is occurring in an organization. In practice, many organizations that think they are implementing TQM, including many healthcare institutions, fail to meet the full spirit of Bemowski's definition. Many fall short on policies directed to "long-term success," often substituting policies designed for short-term success. Others fail to include "all members of an organization," restricting participation to only a part of an organization. Still others fail to make the necessary changes in organization "culture," invariably putting new wine in old bottles. As a result, it is difficult for dispassionate researchers to measure whether TQM works empirically, since there are many organizations that claim to use TQM but do so in an abbreviated form that often does not do justice to the process.

## What are TQM Management Principles?

TQM management principles include the following—

1. It says that the primary objective of an organization is to meet the needs of its "customers" by providing quality goods and services, and to continually improve them. In the non-profit organization context, customers include not only the direct recipients of services, such as clients, but the organization's board, elected and appointed government officials, the media, and the general public.

2. It instills in all organization members an *esprit de corps* that assures them that *having quality* as the number one goal is an important tenet. Organizational members are responsible for quality, even if it is related to an issue beyond the scope of his or her job. Eliminating the "it's not my job" mentality becomes an achievable organizational objective.

3. It continuously searches for ways to improve every activity, program, and process. It does so by constantly seeking feedback from its customers, and promoting suggestions from all sources, both externally and internally, on how to improve.

4. It rewards quality, not only internally, but from its suppliers. It recognizes that poor quality from its collaborators, be they suppliers or other organizations, affects the organization's quality.

5. It recognizes that staff must receive continuous training to improve their work performance.

6. It encourages all aspects of the organization to work as a team to solve problems and meet customer needs rather than competing against each other.

7. It empowers workers at every level, and permits them to be actively engaged in decisions that affect the organization, and to constantly look for ways to improve it.

8. It permits employees the opportunity to have pride in what they produce for the organization and to see the fruits of their labor measured in the quality of the service they provide rather than just having a paycheck.

9. It promotes a planning process that is geared toward continuously improving quality in *everything* the organization does.

A list of principles of quality management compiled by Dr. W. Edwards Deming, the man considered by many to be the founder of the modern quality movement, can be found in Appendix B.

In his 1993 book *Total Quality Management in Human Service Organizations*, Professor Martin points out that conventional management philosophy upholds that:

1. profits and "bottom line" are the number one driving force in management.

2. competition is preferable to cooperation.

3. change occurs in large pieces rather than incrementally and slowly.

4. American organization leaders engage in "cowboy management" that involves entrepreneurial leaders fighting bureaucracies to make changes.

5. management takes action to change things only when things go wrong.

Martin points out that TQM directly conflicts with each of these principles. *Quality* is the number one driving force in management. *Cooperation* is preferable to competition. TQM enhances *slow, incremental change* that involves *continuous quality improvement*, and change is based on *careful planning* rather than seat-of-the-pants instinct by the manager.

He also explains that TQM and "teams" go together.

"TQM attempts to mix what might be called the 'scientific management' perspective (managing with data) with the human relations school—understanding interpersonal and group dynamics. This is accomplished by having teams work with data," he says.

James H. Saylor in his 1996 book, *TQM Simplified, A Practical Guide (Second Edition)*, levels an eleven-count indictment of conventional management practices. He says that traditional management seeks the *quick fix* rather than long-term solutions, "*firefights*" rather than adopts a disciplined approach to continuous improvement, *operates traditionally* rather than seeking innovation and creativity, *makes improvements randomly* rather than continuously, *places a priority on inspection* rather than prevention of defects, *decides using personal opinions* rather than facts, *allocates money and technology* for improvements rather than maximizing people power, *controls workers* rather than empowering workers, *looks at individual performance* rather than team performance, *is motivated by profit* rather than customer satisfaction, and *relies on programs* rather than a never-ending quest for quality. TQM addresses each of these issues.

**The Baldrige Award and TQM**

Perhaps the single most influential factor in accelerating the adoption of TQM principles in mainstream American business organizations has been the Malcolm Baldrige Award. The guidelines for the award explicitly recognize the concepts of TQM. Malcolm Baldrige served as Secretary of Commerce in the Reagan Administration from 1981 until his death in 1987 in a rodeo accident. Congress memorialized his interest in quality with a "National Quality Award" in his name, administered by a public/private partnership. The criteria for the award were put together by a panel of quality experts, and TQM principles serve as the basis for granting the award.

The award criteria are judged on a 1,000 point scale of performance in seven major categories: leadership, information and analysis, planning, human resource utilization, quality assurance, quality results, and customer satisfaction. The final two criteria comprise about half of the points. While results are important, the award is designed to make applicants also focus on the conditions and processes that led to the results. Within just a few years, the Baldrige Quality Award became one of the most highly sought after honors of the business community, although in recent years, according to some who should know, it has lost a bit of its luster.

In 1992, The United Way of America developed an analogous award for non-profit human service agencies, recognizing that quality improvement is just as important, if not more so, in charities as private business. Known as the Excellence in Service Quality Award (ESQA), 501(c)(3) charities are eligible for four levels of recognition, with judging and criteria patterned after the Baldrige Award. Unlike its business counterpart, the ESQAs are non-competitive in that there is no limit on the number of winners in any given year.

**History of the TQM Movement**

The TQM movement is attributed mostly to the work of three gurus: W. Edwards Deming, Joseph Juran, and Philip Crosby. Among other major contributors have been Armand Feigenbaum, Kaoru Ishikawa, Genichi Taguchi, Peter Drucker, Tom Peters, H. James Harrington, and A. Richard Shores.

Dr. Deming, a statistician, pointed out "seven deadly diseases" of American organizations, which include lacking meaningful strategic planning, maximizing short-term profits, basing remuneration on individual performance, accepting high medical costs, refusing to discourage managers from leaving, basing decisions on numbers that do not factor in quality information, and having excessive costs related to warranty of their products. Perhaps the most oft-quoted paper on the principles of TQM is Deming's *On Some Statistical Aids Toward Economic Production.*

Other than the painful fact that Deming's principles have been adopted by Japanese business and Japan achieved a major competitive advantage over those in the United States that lagged in accepting Deming's perspective on quality, Deming probably would have been dismissed as a cantankerous eccentric.

Joseph Juran served in both government and the private sector. In 1979, he established the Juran Institute. He is credited with the definition of quality as "fitness to use," meaning that the customer could do with the product what was intended. Juran described five dimensions of fitness to use: quality of design, quality of conformance, availability, safety, and field use. He applied a systematic dissection of the product's lifecycle cradle to grave—from conception to design, manufacturing, inspection and test, and distribution—and used statistical techniques to improve all aspects of these five dimensions. Juran theorized that managing for quality consists of three basic quality-oriented processes, a quality trilogy: quality planning, quality control, and quality improvement.

Quality planning consists of creating a process to accomplish quality objectives under the operational constraints. Juran contends that poor planning is responsible for the waste that occurs once production begins. Quality control is the function that describes quality management once planning has been completed and operations begin. Finally, quality improvement is the endeavor that seeks constant improvement in quality. Juran notes that there is an analogous trilogy in the financial management process: budgeting, cost/expense control, and cost reduction.

Quality planning consists of—

- identifying the customer (both internal and external)
- determining his or her needs
- developing products and services and features of products/services the customer needs
- designing and building the process that produces those products/services in a way that meets quality goals "and do so at a minimum combined cost"—an important distinction compared to Deming.

Quality control requires choosing units of measurements, establishing performance standards, measuring actual performance, and taking action to correct any deficiencies from those standards.

Quality improvement consists of diagnosing what is keeping quality standards low and finding remedies, and consolidating the gains in quality improvement.

Juran's view is that American managers are strong on quality control and, by a large margin, make it their top priority. However, they are weak on quality planning and quality improvement.

Juran has a prescription for improving quality, which typically begins by establishing a quality planning council within the organization. The task of the council is to—

- Establish corporate quality policies
- Establish corporate quality goals; review quality goals of divisions and major functions

- Establish corporate quality plans; review divisional and functional plans
- Review quality performance against plans and goals
- Revise the managerial merit rating system to reflect performance against quality goals.

## Philip Crosby

Philip Crosby is one generation younger than Juran and Deming, and had worked as International Telephone and Telegraph's (ITT) Vice President of Quality before becoming a private consultant, lecturer, and author on quality issues. In 1986, he set up the Crosby Quality College, which taught TQM principles to tens of thousands of executives and managers. Crosby focused on changing attitudes and behaviors in the workforce to instill an attitude in workers that would eliminate careless mistakes that created costly rework.

Crosby asserts that American management typically speaks in quantitative terms when talking about sales, employee compensation, inventory, budget, and about almost everything else—other than quality. This is despite measurable standards being available, which Crosby points out were developed by General Electric in the 1950s. Crosby was perhaps the first to put a "cost" on quality, aggregating costs of rework, scrap, warranty, inspection, and test.

Crosby's writing on quality improvement is practical, and provides a guide for managers committed to calculating and reducing their COQ (cost of quality). Using golf analogies (not a bad thing to do considering his audience), Crosby passionately doesn't speak down to his audience, but uses a folksy style to introduce his 14-point program (each with an action program and an "accomplishment" section explaining why) for quality management:

1. Obtain and enforce commitment to quality improvement by management.
2. Create a quality improvement team with folks from each department.
3. Find acceptable ways to measure quality in each department.
4. Evaluate the cost of quality.
5. Educate all workers about the cost of quality (or more ap-

propriately, the cost of non-quality).

6. Facilitate corrective action by having workers at all levels communicate to management remedies for improving quality.
7. Establish a Zero Defects Program.
8. Provide training so that all supervisors buy into quality management.
9. Create a "Zero Defects Day" and make the commitment to ZD long-lasting.
10. Establish quality goals.
11. Ask workers to describe problems that keep them from performing error-free work, and respond to these within 24 hours.
12. Establish an award program to recognize outstanding achievement and those who meet their goals. (Crosby suggests recognition rather than cash as the award.)
13. Establish Quality Councils to report on the status of the quality management program and ideas for action.
14. Start over again every 12-18 months, because turnover and changing conditions wipe out progress made in education and training.

If major American companies were slow to react to the realization that the stellar economic success in Japan was being attributed to TQM, healthcare institutions were a decade behind the curve. Not surprisingly, healthcare institutions, particularly hospitals, have been at the vanguard of TQM adoption by non-profit organizations. One reason for TQM to finally catch on is that there has been a major transformation of the hospital industry.

First, large for-profit conglomerates have built empires consisting of newly acquired hospital chains, such as Columbia/HCA Healthcare Corporation and Tenet Healthcare Corporation. Hundreds of hospitals have converted from non-profit orientation to for-profit. Even those that have not converted are still subject to the financial and competitive pressures that resulted in hundreds of hospital mergers during the 1980s and 1990s.

Decreased Medicare and Medicaid reimbursements by the Health Care Financing Administration (HCFA); managed care; cut-throat marketing efforts; strong cost containment pressures from insurance companies; the high cost of, and the competition for, medical technology; and required public disclosure of hospital costs and clinical outcomes have been among the trends that have changed the face of the healthcare industry. Other factors have been increased consumer competition (health care users had new incentives to shop around for medical care); major restructuring of the third-party payment system by both government (Medicaid, Medicare) and insurance companies; and government regulation of managed care practices.

Reading the literature on TQM in healthcare organizations, one comes to realize that TQM is not being implemented to any great degree in a holistic, system-wide, full-blown way, but rather piecemeal, and in a manner that is targeted to reducing cost. This is not consistent with the TQM philosophy, and the potential benefits of this management strategy may be missed as a result.

Managed care has revolutionized the healthcare industry in recent years. Healthcare practitioners view this revolution in practical terms, for the most part. TQM is seen by some practitioners as a means to objectively measure quality, which is important to both third-party payers (such as insurance companies) and patients. Hospital executives have come to realize that quality control can reduce costs.

TQM principles are finding their way into non-profit settings other than healthcare, such as community centers, arts organizations, and human services agencies. Focusing on the needs of the "customer" rather than on the "bottom line" is a value that the non-profit sector should feel comfortable with compared to its for-profit counterparts. When a non-profit organization's leadership becomes excited about TQM, it can become contagious, provided that the behaviors of the leaders are consistent with their words. When it "happens," those in a TQM environment notice the difference, whether they work there or benefit from the organization's services. Workers feel empowered. Clients notice a positive difference in staff attitudes. Everyone associated with the organization feels good about it.

## Tips for Implementing TQM

1. *Diagnose the present state of your organization.* This includes a scan of client satisfaction, attitudes and morale of staff, and the standing of the organization in your "market." Assess the extent of commitment by top executives to a formal change process, if the organizational culture will support

change, and if TQM is a "good fit" compared to alternative change management strategies.

2. *Design the TQM Program.* Decide who will be in charge of leading the effort. Decide the roles of staff and outside consultants. Choose the particular TQM implementation model, and consider modifications required. Look at how communications will have to be improved and expanded. Decide how stakeholders such as clients and funders will participate. Assess what changes need to be made in your mission statement, vision statement, and values statement.

3. *Develop the TQM System.* Prepare and distribute training materials, and conduct training. Implement a pilot program to demonstrate the techniques, if appropriate. Quantify current baseline outcomes and prepare strategic outcome goals. Identify resources to allocate to the project, and consider risks and costs involved as a result of potential disruptions or failure. Put together a record-keeping and data-collection system, work procedures, and policies to promote quality. Designate problem-solving teams.

4. *Install the Program.* Continue training, and implement the TQM program. Collect and analyze data and use it to make mid-course corrections and incrementally improve processes.

5. *Evaluate the Program.* Measure progress against the strategic goals, and periodically perform an audit of the effectiveness of the program.

## Up Close: James Benté

James Benté serves as Vice President, Quality, for the Valley Health System in Beaver, Pennsylvania, which includes Sewickley Valley Hospital (SVH) and the Medical Center, Beaver—two community hospitals located in western Pennsylvania. In that position and a parallel position with Volunteer Hospitals of America, Benté has been on the front lines of the quality revolution and has seen it from a non-profit organizational perspective. SVH began a formal TQM program in 1989 and has realized a progressive return on its initial investment in this change management strategy. Over the years, significant improvements in quality management have led to increased customer satisfaction, decreased operating costs, and enhanced employee satisfaction, Benté reports. Several years ago, SVH was presented the Pittsburgh Quality Award by the Pittsburgh Quality Network, sponsored by the Chamber of Commerce.

"It is not really true that the non-profit sector, and especially healthcare, has not been focused on quality issues (as has been alleged)," he says. " Rather, non-profit organizations do not have a good understanding of how to appropriately address and make quality happen." For example, he says that in the healthcare sector, quality assessment was a retrospective process, and was viewed as a way to assure quality.

"It is only a recent development that prospective rather than retrospective quality control, such as process design and real time process control, has made a significant impact. Simply put, we have always been concerned about quality; we simply did not know how to effectively deal with it," he says.

Benté suggests that some of the same factors that make quality important in the for-profit sector lend themselves to the non-profit sector as well. He sees the competition of the market as a driving force behind the movement for quality in the healthcare sector.

"It is important for hospitals to maintain customer loyalty and achieve effective utilization of scarce resources, just as in the for-profit sector," he maintains. "This is especially true in healthcare today, where the choice of the healthcare provider is often driven by the insurer who bases purchasing decisions on financial and outcome data."

Benté relates the story of how TQM was first implemented at SVH.

"The first efforts involved educating and securing the commitment and participation of the board of directors, physician leadership, and all senior management," he recalls. The next step was formal training in quality management techniques provided by Philip Crosby Associates. This training involved each manager attending a 4-day program known as Quality Improvement Process Management College (QIPM) in order to understand how to effectively change the organization's culture and how to implement processes that would support the employees.

"There were also several senior and middle managers identified to attend a 4-day train-the-trainer course in *Quality Education System* (QES)," Benté remembers, explaining that QES is a 20-hour course taught over 10 weeks, and was provided to all of the hospital's managers and supervisors. Physicians were provided with a 6-hour course, *Quality Management for the Medical Staff* (QMMS). The general staff of the facility received a 4-hour course titled *Quality Awareness Experience.*

"The goal of this education was first to provide a common framework and language within the organization and second, to provide individuals with basic problem-solving and problem-prevention tools and techniques," he observes. He says that another key aspect of the process was the implementation of a system that prioritized and sanctioned teams to deal with system-wide problems.

Benté is a true believer when it comes to touting the benefits of TQM.

"Valley Health System remains a very viable organization, with high customer satisfaction and community support," Benté says proudly. "In 1998, when other healthcare organizations were having their financial viability questioned, we had our bonds upgraded by three of the major bond-rating agencies. We have just completed a survey by our accreditation organization, and both campuses have preliminarily scored in the mid-nineties."

What advice can he offer non-profit executives with respect to improving the quality of their organizations' services? He offers six suggestions. "First, understand that the way to increased customer satisfaction, productivity, and product/service reliability is by reducing variation. In order to achieve this, the organization must use real time, online data, and subject it to appropriate analysis using tools such as Statistical Process Control.

"Second, truly understand what the customer wants, and then focus on those aspects of the process/products that are most important in meeting those needs.

"Third, do not underestimate the knowledge and creativity of the staff, and their importance in customer satisfaction.

"Fourth, ninety-five percent of the problems an organization faces are due to systems and not people. Managers must remember that every process is uniquely designed to deliver the results it produces. Therefore, the focus must truly be on controlling processes, and not people.

"Fifth, the vast majority of individuals come to work wanting to do a good job, and make a contribution. If employees start to become disenchanted with the job, it is important to look at what management is doing wrong and why the organizational systems are failing the employees.

"And finally, give the management change time to work. Dr. Deming once said that it takes 10 years of change for every 50 years of entrenched organizational culture. We are a quick fix, quick results society, and not seeing immediate results often causes organizations to give up on a solid strategy."

# 3
# Introduction to Business Process Reengineering

If your heart stops beating and you keel over breathlessly, a professionally trained medical professional can often revive you by administering CPR. But if it's your organization's heart that fails, BPR, administered by professionally-trained consultants or by those within an organization, is increasingly becoming the TLA ("three-letter acronym") of choice for cutting-edge managers, and a successor to TQM as the latest management bromide for reviving comatose organizations.

Business Process Reengineering is defined by Michael Hammer, the W. Edwards Deming of BPR, as "the fundamental rethinking and radical redesign of business processes to achieve dramatic improvements in critical measures of performance (cost, quality, capital, service and speed)."

The fanatical interest in Total Quality Management peaked in the 1980s, but its once-pervasive influence seems to have waned in recent years. One of the reasons often given for its apparent decline in the United States is that the philosophy of slow, incremental, and continuous improvement is generally inconsistent with American culture. Perhaps this is so; American organizational leaders are perceived as more impatient to see tangible results of their business management interventions compared to their Asian, African, and European counterparts. They want to see quantum leaps of measurable improvement rather than the tortoise-paced improvement promised by TQM advocates. The tenure of many organizational leaders is short; many CEOs come and go before TQM is fully implemented and showing results.

This new management technique was brought to prominence by an article in the July-August 1990 *Harvard Business Review* by Hammer entitled *Re-engineering Work: Don't Automate, Obliterate.* Hammer, the President of a Cambridge, Massachusetts-based information technology company, promised revolutionary and spectacular short-term returns by abandoning continuous improvement in favor of radical and dramatic change. Hammer suggested that TQM falls short in helping companies meet the challenge of global competition in that it takes too long to see the results. The article reinvigorated a business community becoming frustrated with TQM, and heralded the business process reengineering movement.

Hammer's article was not simply an academic exercise. He based his article on a pattern he noticed about what some companies did to dramatically improve business processes.

Hammer's primary thesis is that conventional business practices evolved from ideas formulated in the 18th century at the beginning of the Industrial Revolution relating to division of labor. These ideas made sense at the time, when there was not the skilled, professional labor force and sophistication of information technology there is today. An employee could be trained to perform a single task and perform it well repetitively, coordinated by skilled managers who controlled the workers. Organizations manufacturing and selling goods found it efficient to divide themselves into bureaus and departments, with written and unwritten policies and rules providing guidance to each worker who exercised little, if any, independent decision-making authority. Typically under the conventional business organization model, an order from a customer had to be passed through a gauntlet of bureaus and workers before it was fulfilled (e.g., a sales person to obtain the order, a credit department to authorize the credit, an inventory department to see if the product ordered was available, an accounting department to prepare the invoice, a shipping department to ship the product, an accounts receivable department to process the check, and a returns department to handle returns).

The concept of reengineering is not new, as illustrated by a case history related by Raymond L. Manganelli and Mark M. Klein in their 1994 book, *The Reengineering Handbook*. They tell the story of William Sowder Sims, who came up with some breakthrough, innovative ideas on improving the accuracy of naval artillery. Sims came up with the idea of "continuous aim firing," making adjustment in artillery gear ratios and moving the gun sight so an artillery shell fired from a ship would have, as he calculated, an improved accuracy of 3,000%. The idea, however, threatened the existing structure and culture of the Navy, in which navigators held the most important positions. As a result, Sims' ideas were either ignored or rejected until President Theodore Roosevelt read about the proposal in a letter from Sims, and ordered that Sims' report be distributed to every officer in the Navy. The changes were made, accuracy did indeed improve 3,000%, and the course of naval history was changed forever.

Manganelli and Klein draw several important conclusions from this story. First, reengineering is not a new concept, but the willingness of organization executives to apply the techniques organization-wide is new. Second, innovations that make quantum improvements require vision, which involves "thinking outside the box." Third, the greatest obstacle to these radical breakthroughs is organizational resistance to change. Fourth, reengineering requires approval from the top to effect breakthrough change.

Fifth, the change agent in reengineering is usually someone who is not part of the organizational power structure. Sixth, there are limits to benchmarking (see Chapter 4), and there still may be opportunities to find those elusive innovations that improve performance many times over existing levels. Seventh, reengineering is an effective strategy whether an organization is teetering on the brink of competitive disaster, or whether it is the top dog. Eighth, perseverance is required to implement radical change, because most proposals to implement radical change must overcome substantial organizational resistance. And finally, the point of reengineering is to find dramatic improvement rather than incremental improvement.

A major strategy involved with BPR efforts is to look at a business process that has many tasks that have been performed by several specialists. Replace the specialists with generalists (or retrain the specialists to become generalists) who can handle all of the tasks of the process and have access to all of the information they need to perform *all* of the tasks.

"At the heart of business reengineering lies the notion of discontinuous thinking—identifying and abandoning the outdated rules and fundamental assumptions that underlie operations," Hammer wrote. The phrase "thinking outside the box" was not invented to describe BPR, but is often used in describing how managers should be flinging away conventional thinking about business processes, and considering redesign options that are not politically correct and go beyond traditional and standard business protocol.

In two subsequent books about reengineering (*Reengineering the Corporation*, co-authored by James Champy and *The Reengineering Revolution*, co-authored by Steven A. Standon), Hammer expanded upon his *Harvard Business Review* article. The first book became a *New York Times* bestseller, selling more than 1.7 million copies in its first 18 months, and it was translated into 19 languages.

Business leaders were not only reading it, but launching ambitious reengineering projects. American business's ardor for TQM was being inexorably replaced by a fascination with BPR by the middle of the last decade of the 20th century. Hammer's philosophy has turned him into a highly sought-after speaker on the business lecture circuit, and he commands fees ranging from $30,000-$50,000 per speech, among the highest in the industry for all types of speakers.

Hammer points out that information technology and automation have not been used to their potential. Organizations tend to use computers to speed up existing work processes rather than redesigning the work processes to take advantage of the technology. Since the work processes (usually defined in the business literature as the related tasks that achieve a particular business outcome) were designed before the new technology became available, they are inherently inefficient. Hammer calls for a radical change in the way businesses operate—start from scratch and redesign the work processes, using the advantages of information technology.

"It is time to stop paving the cow paths," he wrote in his seminal *Harvard Business Review* article, a line that has become a mantra for BPR adherents.

BPR requires a new way of thinking. Unlike TQM, which requires the involvement of everyone in the organization, BPR is necessarily implemented from the top. It is the zero-based budgeting of business processes, asserting that, at least theoretically, the past should have no bearing on what is planned for the future. It makes the assumption that organizations have evolved incrementally, reflecting a history of culture, tradition, technology, and customer needs that may not be particularly relevant today. BPR suggests that managers step out of the constraints of their current physical plant, work processes, organizational charts, and procedures and rules and look at how the work would be performed if they were starting from scratch.

BPR requires an organizational leader to step back and answer the question: If I were building this organization today from scratch, knew what I know now, had the technology and human resources that I have now, and the customer needs that I have now, would I still be doing things the same way? More often than not, the answer is "no!" In the non-profit environment, this might mean redesigning data collection and reporting, client intake, billing, purchasing, and every other process.

In many cases, new technology is available that will enable efficiencies. For example, a human service agency may receive a telephone call from a client requesting even a minimal change in service as a result of some change in circumstances. The person answering the telephone may have to put the person on hold and call the client's caseworker, who has the client's case file. The caseworker may have to put the person on hold and check with the supervisor for a decision on whether to waive a rule, and the supervisor may have to meet with the caseworker in order to make the decision.

Following BPR, the person answering the telephone for the agency may be able to pull up the case file on a computer screen and be preauthorized to approve a change in services within a constraint programmed into the computer by the agency. Or the person answering the telephone may be able to give the caller technical advice on how to solve a problem by searching a "frequently asked questions" file on a computer screen that previously was routinely transferred to a technical specialist.

Another way of looking at this is that everyone in the organization is functioning solely on his or her part of a process rather than on the objective of the organization. The receptionist answers the telephone. The case manager holds the file for a particular set of clients. The supervisor makes decisions authorizing variances from agency rules. BPR permits a work process to change so that the true objective of the process—responding to the client's needs—does not require the intervention of several people in the organization. The revolutionary advance of information technology permits this.

With the use of networked computers and an educated labor force, it is possible for a single person to process and troubleshoot an entire order that previously may have required being passed serially from person to person in the organization, taking many days to complete. And the probability of an error under the old method multiplies the more hands are involved.

In Hammer's words:

> *Conventional process structures are fragmented and piecemeal, and they lack the integration necessary to maintain quality and service. They are the breeding grounds for tunnel vision, as people tend to substitute the narrow goals of their particular department for the larger goals of the process as a whole. When work is handed off from person to person and unit to unit, delays and errors are inevitable. Accountability blurs, and critical issues fall between the cracks. Moreover, no one sees enough of the big picture to be able to respond quickly to new situations.*

Hammer proposed as a first principle using modern technology to redesign work processes rather than work tasks, concentrating on permitting a single person to achieve a desired outcome/objective. For example, in the context of a non-profit human services organization, each client would receive a case manager who is responsible for all contact with the client, who is empowered within pre-set constraints to allocate resources of the organization to that client, and whose supervisor acts more as an advisor and consultant.

A second principle is that those who use the output of a process also perform the process. For example, instead of having a purchasing department make purchases of pencils and paper clips for the accounting department and other departments, the accounting department orders its own pencils and paper clips and other "inexpensive and nonstrategic" purchases. Doing so eliminates the counterproductive situation where the cost of making a purchase can exceed the cost of the products being purchased, and it avoids delays and errors.

For example, there is intense competition among mail order office supply companies. They send out catalogs offering discount office supplies and provide 800 numbers, no-hassle returns, and immediate credit. Does it really make sense for a purchasing department to handle routine office supply purchases for an entire organization when economies of scale are minimal? Many organizations require their employees to fill out a form for routine office supply purchases, have the forms approved by someone else, and then submit the form to a purchasing department for processing. Simply permitting departments to have an office supplies budget and authorization to purchase their own office supplies from pre-approved discount supply houses is a form of business process reengineering.

The layers of bureaucracy are cut, the office supplies can arrive the following day without any unnecessary paperwork, and the staff/staff time for processing these purchases is eliminated. Employees feel empowered when they don't have to grovel with someone from another department to buy paper clips that, as is often the case, arrive on their desks weeks later, and in the incorrect size and amount, through the fault of neither the person requesting the supplies nor the vendor.

A third principle is that those in the organization who collect information should also be the ones who process it. For example, when the public relations department wants to send out its newsletter to a mailing list, it should be able to generate the mailing labels itself rather than having to make a request to a data processing department.

Fourth, Hammer suggests that organization resources that were decentralized should be treated as centralized, utilizing information technology to bring them together. A college with several satellite campuses, for example, could link its bursars so that a student making a payment at either the main office or a satellite campus would have the payment show up in the records of the registrars of all of the campuses.

Fifth, disparate parts of an organization should be electronically linked to promote coordination.

Sixth, let those who perform the work make the decisions, thereby flattening the pyramidal management layers and eliminating the bureaucracy and delay that slows down a decision-making process.

Seventh, use relational databases and other technology to collect and store information only once, eliminating both redundancy and error.

BPR is paradoxically both consistent with, and diametrically opposite to, TQM. Many see it as an evolution of TQM rather than a repudiation of it. As pointed out in a 1993 book by T. H. Davenport, *Process Innovation, Reengineering Work Through In-*

*formation Technology*, TQM and BPR have similar roots and are both driven by the needs of customers, but diverge in their practice. TQM, for example, provides for incremental improvement, while BPR results in radical, discontinuous improvement. TQM makes changes to existing processes, while BPR starts out with a clean slate. TQM is a continuous process, while BPR is a one-time redesign. TQM involves all organizational employees and requires commitment from the bottom up, while BPR typically is a top-down management initiative. TQM involves moderate risk to the organization, but BPR involves high risk (although proponents recommend that a trial run of the process occurs before completely replacing an existing process). TQM utilizes statistical process control to enable workers to judge when to intervene in a process, while BPR utilizes the benefits of information technology to empower workers.

According to a 1996 article by Dr. Yogesh Malhotra, 70% of business reengineering projects fail. He attributes this to three reasons: lack of management commitment and leadership, unrealistic scope and expectations, and resistance to change. Indeed, BPR is viewed by many workers as a euphemism for organizational downsizing, since most BPR projects have as goals the elimination of layers of management and other workers. BPR suggests a radical and dramatic change in business processes. Employees are empowered to do jobs once performed by several, assisted by information technology.

Even Hammer, in his first book, suggests that 50-70% of BPR efforts don't achieve the desired performance breakthroughs, although he suggests that rate of success is dependent upon the quality, intensity, and intelligence of the BPR effort. Why do efforts fail? Hammer and his colleagues say that there is one major underlying factor: the people doing the project don't know what they are doing and don't implement BPR techniques correctly based on practical experience.

Generally, BPR often enables a single person to perform all of the steps in a process by using information technology. One byproduct of BPR is that the need for many employees may be eliminated. This saves a lot of money for organizations. And it has the consequence of terrorizing a workforce. At the conclusion of a BPR implementation, there are often "winners" and "losers." Some of the losers may be out of a job despite being loyal and highly skilled employees. Organizations have invested heavily in finding and retaining these employees, and it is good business sense not to squander this resource. From a non-profit organization perspective, humanizing the BPR process is consistent with values of non-profit organizations. Even for-profit companies that have reorganized find it to be good business to treat their employees humanely, and minimize the pain and suffering that often accompanies BPR efforts.

## BPR Implementation

There are several BPR implementation strategies that have been developed. Summarizing some of the more popular strategies, a BPR implementation plan should include—

1. articulating the organization's goals and vision for the future, and quantifying objectives
2. identifying all business processes
3. benchmarking all of those processes (see Chapter 4)
4. performing an environmental analysis to identify economic, legal, political, technical, social, and other external forces
5. reviewing customer needs, complaints, and suggestions and using surveys and focus groups to collect more customer input
6. brainstorming by senior staff on how to improve business processes and meet customer needs regardless of the constraints of current design
7. developing a consensus among management on a plan to redesign business processes.
8. developing a timetable for redesign
9. designating a management team responsible for implementing the redesign, and motivating that team
10. designing a pilot for each redesigned business process, and testing that pilot
11. conducting staff training to implement the redesign
12. communicating to all employees the goals and status of the project
13. implementing the redesign
14. evaluating the redesign
15. minimizing the collateral damage to employees who are no longer needed as a result of the redesign
16. implementing continuous improvement to capitalize on the benefits of the BPR intervention.

## Up Close: Dr. Larry Kennedy

Non-profit management consultant Dr. Larry Kennedy, author of *Quality Management in the Nonprofit World*, was introduced to quality management during his many years in the aerospace industry. Prior to becoming a consultant, he held responsible management positions with the National Aeronautics and Space Administration, a federal government leader in the development and implementation of system-wide quality management.

He served as an assistant pastor of the church to which Philip Crosby, one of the founders of the TQM movement, belonged, and was hired by Crosby to manage his philanthropic contributions. This serendipitous contact with one of the patriarchs of quality management was the beginning of more than two decades of a close personal and professional relationship, which continues today. Eventually, Kennedy not only took all of the non-profit management courses Crosby offered at his Quality College, but eventually became a certified instructor there and a "Johnny Appleseed" for Crosby's philosophy. A resident of Orlando, he received his Ph.D. from the Union Institute in 1990.

Most of Kennedy's book, published in 1991 by Jossey-Bass Publications, is geared to advocating the lessons Crosby teaches, but from a non-profit perspective. It is one of the most readable books on the market, offering practical advice to non-profit executives interested in quality issues.

Kennedy has observed differences between the non-profit sector and for-profit sector with respect to their perspectives on quality issues, but feels it is a myth that the for-profit sector cares more about providing quality products and services.

"Those who manage non-profit organizations are more attuned to the issues of quality as it regards the efficacy of their services, but they have generally been committed less to the organizational disciplines of quality management," Kennedy observes. "NPOs have always been far more sensitive to the core values of their clients and the need to understand their requirements than most for-profit companies. They also possess a consistent attitude of serving the needs of people. But, too often they are willing to indulge themselves in the good feelings they have about doing good things at the expense of doing them well."

He points out that non-profit organizations have a tendency to be unable to accept the accountability of Quality Management, excusing themselves from the data collection and paperwork required for formal TQM programs because of the goodness of their mission. In contrast, for-profit companies are cold-blooded about the need to conform to customers' requirements in order to maintain market share and remain profitable.

"Non-profit organizations sometimes act like undisciplined but loving shepherds, while for-profit organizations are harvesting fleece," he analogizes.

"I believe non-profit executives can compete with their for-profit counterparts on the technical side of management," he asserts. "They are usually making personal sacrifices to forward their mission that the for-profit manager would never dream of doing." But unlike most for-profit businesses, he believes, non-profits chiefly deliver human services, and thus have a stewardship role over vulnerable people that should encourage their organizations to emphasize quality.

Kennedy laments the isolated incidents of quality failure of non-profits that are often highlighted in the media for the public to see, and that adversely affect the public's perception of the non-profit sector. "Every time I see an article in a newspaper or a piece on TV about the failure of a non-profit organization to hold itself accountable for moral, ethical, or financial mistakes, I know that clients have suffered at their hands—and these failures do not occur in a vacuum," he says. "Not only will the clients and the constituents of the headlined organization suffer, but everyone in the community who offers similar services suffers along with them."

Over the years, Kennedy has advised more than 100 non-profit organizations on improving their management, particularly emphasizing the philosophy of Crosby and his colleagues at the Crosby Quality College. Where has any resistance come from implementing programs to improve quality within organizations?

"Resistance always comes from the centers of influence within an organization who feel threatened by the routine accountability of Quality Management," he points out. "Some people just do not like being told that they can do things better. Instead of embracing the search for the causes of errors as the search for recovery of hidden treasure, they resist it as an intruder."

Through his book, consulting work, and courses at the Crosby Quality College, Kennedy is steadfast in his support for TQM as a management philosophy, and believes it fits well with the goals and objectives of virtually all non-profit organizations.

"The benefits of TQM far outweigh the drawbacks," he asserts. "Non-profit organizations must focus on increasing the reliability of their services, and TQM helps with that aim."

But implementing Quality Management into an organization will either raise it to new levels of effectiveness or destroy it, depending on the ability of the CEO to involve him or herself in the processes of implementation, holding him or herself and their colleagues equally accountable, he warns. "An organization which establishes the language of Quality Management without the practices of Quality Management will soon succumb to the sword of hypocrisy."

In the effort to adopt change, the CEO must also have the commitment of the board to make quality management a practice rather than just a slogan, he says. "The board's role is to make sure that the stated values of an organization are consistent with their policies, procedures, and practiced values," he says. "The board should be auditors who follow the adage of the famous Russian proverb 'trust, but verify,' shamelessly pursuing the facts about their organization's performance."

And what is Kennedy's "bottom line" advice to non-profit organizations?

"Non-profit organizations should never be satisfied with any standard for the delivery of services which considers a defect in a service delivered to a client as acceptable," he counsels. "That's a 'zero defects' attitude and it will pay many dividends."

# 4
# Introduction to Benchmarking and Best Practices
### *by Jason Saul*

Over the past 20 years, Corporate America has been doing something the non-profit sector has only just begun: pushing the envelope of its own performance, solving difficult problems with amazing rapidity and generating a never-ending stream of innovations. Corporations have been able to do this in part by learning from each other's inventions. On a consistent basis, companies seek out the best new ideas from top performing competitors and copy them:

> *Ford and Chrysler did it when they adapted Japanese automobile manufacturing processes and design concepts.*
>
> *MBNA America did it when it issued a Platinum Visa Card based on the success of the American Express Platinum Card.*
>
> *United Airlines did it when it began offering its last-minute E-fares on the Internet after seeing the success of American Airlines in unloading leftover seats.*

This process of systematically identifying and adapting other people's successful ideas to improve one's own performance is called "benchmarking." Benchmarking allows any organization to make today's state-of-the-art into tomorrow's industry standard.

Benchmarking holds tremendous potential for the non-profit sector. Non-profits, too, are corporations with defined goals,

*The material in Chapter 4 of this publication is from the* Benchmarking Workbook for Nonprofit Organizations, *a work-in-progress by Jason A. Saul. Copyright 1998 Jason A. Saul. This chapter is part of a larger work by the author to be released by the Wilder Publishing Center, St. Paul, Minnesota, in 1999. Used with permission. For more information on this book and other Wilder Foundation publications, call 1-800-274-6024, or visit their Web site at www.wilder.org.*

measurable results, and mutual problems. Currently, most non-profits seek to learn new ways of solving problems through an array of conferences, technical assistance programs, newsletters, seminars, and consultants. Now, benchmarking offers non-profit organizations a new tool to solve problems and improve performance by learning from each other's successes, innovations, and creative ideas.

## So What is Benchmarking?

Benchmarking is a term that was originally used by land surveyors to mark reference points (buildings, rocks, landmarks) measuring the distance from a particular spot. Setting a benchmark told you how far away you were from a certain reference point. Similarly, organizations set benchmarks, or goals, and use those reference points to measure how close they are to achieving them. In addition to telling your organization where it stands with regard to its own goals or mission, benchmarking can also help you *set* those goals in the first place.

One way of understanding benchmarking is to think of it as a way of "getting answers from the back of the book." Benchmarking is reverse-engineering. It is copying from the test of the smartest guy in the class. Unlike in school, in the real-world there is value to such behavior. There is no time to "reinvent the wheel" or reinvent solutions. So what companies have been doing for years, and what governments and non-profits are now starting to do, is just that—copy the best answers or "practices" from the smartest and most successful organizations in their "class." Simply put, benchmarking is a *process* of continuous improvement whereby an organization learns from others who are accomplishing similar objectives in a more efficient, successful, or innovative way.

So how does this relate to the work of non-profit organizations, which don't particularly have a "bottom line"? The answer is that non-profits *do* have a bottom line. The difference is that non-profits have a *performance margin* rather than *profit margin*. In other words, non-profits measure their success not by how much money they make, but by how much of a "difference" they make—how many mouths they feed, how many people they teach, or how many houses they build.

Today, funders are increasingly looking to non-profit organizations to be accountable in ways they never had to be before.

Foundations are requiring evaluations to measure the success of an organization or a program. Management gurus are talking about running non-profits "like a business." The trend is clearly toward making less money go further. Non-profits must innovate in order to survive. Hence the usefulness of a tool such as benchmarking, which helps non-profit managers improve their organization's efficiency at minimal cost.

## Benefits of Benchmarking

### *The Bottom Line vs. The Top Line*

Benchmarking teaches your organization to set its sights higher. Rather than being limited to improving on last year's performance, those who benchmark learn to readjust their sights, setting goals proactively rather than adjusting to them reactively. In this way, benchmarking infuses your organization with an optimistic, forward-thinking mindset, comparing your performance to the best (or the top-line) as opposed to the traditional "bottom-line" approach.

### *Sharpen Your Mission*

Comparing your organization to others highlights similarities as well as differences. But, in order to compare your performance to that of others, your organization must have a keen understanding of what it *really* does (mission) and where it *really* wants to go (goals). In this way, going through the process of benchmarking helps focus an organization while improving it.

### *Identify Your Strengths And Weaknesses*

The careful self-assessment that benchmarking requires of an organization also helps put into perspective what your organization is really good at as compared to others, and where it needs improvement. Sometimes, you can never really know what you need to improve upon until you see someone else doing it better.

### *Build Creativity Into Problem Solving*

A top-down, benchmarking approach allows non-profit managers to consider alternative ways of achieving their organization's mission. By directing your organization to look outside its own unique experience, benchmarking encourages the decision-makers in your organization to be more open-minded in considering solutions. This creativity infuses the entire organization with new ideas and fresh approaches to everyday problems.

***Forge New Alliances***

It can never hurt to build relationships and networks. One of the byproducts of the benchmarking process is the ties that are created among benchmarking partners. What's more, since benchmarking works best with organizations that have similar goals, it has the effect of bringing together groups that are interested in solving the same problems. The ties established through benchmarking often lead to more enduring relationships and future joint endeavors.

***Impress Stakeholders***

Organizations that demonstrate a commitment to tracking their results and improving upon them always impress funders. With increasing corporate support for non-profit endeavors, benchmarking will enable you to speak the language of corporate sponsors. Furthermore, the data that you will gather through the benchmarking process about your own organization, and also about your competitors, will add a new dimension to your annual reports.

## Internal vs. External Benchmarking

There are generally two approaches to benchmarking: internal benchmarking and external benchmarking. *Internal benchmarking* is the process of looking inside your organization, at its own historical performance, and projecting future goals based on that track record. Such planning is very helpful, keeping an organization focused on its goals and setting aggressive targets for employees to work toward. However, one shortfall of *internal benchmarking* is that it doesn't tell you *how* to meet those goals or increase your performance.

*External benchmarking*, on the other hand, involves looking outside your organization, to examine how other organizations designed to meet the same objectives are meeting them in ways that are better, faster, or cheaper. In other words, *external benchmarking* asks, "In your field, who is the 'best' at what they are doing and what makes them so good?" Once those "best practices" are identified, the methods and procedures of your own organization are compared or "benchmarked" against those used by the top-performing firms. The lessons learned from lead organizations are then imported into your organization. The knowledge gained through this process can exponentially increase your organization's performance, establish a proactive rather than a reactive agenda for the future, and help hone your organization's focus.

While both internal and external benchmarking are valuable, this chapter focuses primarily on external benchmarking. The reasons are simple. Most non-profits are already focused on their own internal problems, and consequently, on solving those problems internally. This linear approach to problem-solving confines the universe of solutions to your own in-house staff. External benchmarking encourages non-profits to become more proactive — to think outside the box. Solutions abound throughout the marketplace; in fact, it is likely that many non-profits have already experienced and solved many of the problems your organization is currently facing. Rather than reinventing wheels, or simply spinning them, we suggest learning from others who have done it already, or who are doing it better. Why not? Why not use the cumulative power of many organizations to improve your own organization's performance?

## What Are Best Practices?

If benchmarking is the *process* by which an organization seeks to increase effectiveness by learning from the successes of others, best practices are the *byproducts* of that process. They are the successful innovations or techniques of other top-performing organizations that you wish to learn about through benchmarking. A best practice could be an entire program, like a tuition incentive program to keep inner-city kids in school, or it might be an innovative idea like having a comedian teach safe-driving programs for speeders.

To determine which practices are "best" for your organization, you must first identify precisely and concretely what goals your organization is trying to achieve. This self-examination process is crucial to successful benchmarking; without it, you risk fishing with the wrong bait. There are now plenty of "best practices databases" available that list innovative solutions. However, divorced from the process of benchmarking, best practices are merely orphan ideas. Benchmarking is an *organic* process whereby best practices are borne out of a careful examination of the needs and wants of a particular organization.

Once you have established what you're looking for, the real trick becomes screening out the mediocre programs or ideas from the good ones. Determining what constitutes a best practice is the most challenging part of benchmarking. What makes one practice "better" than another? The answer is—it varies. What's best for one organization may not be best for another. In fact, there is rarely a "one-size-fits-all" solution to a particular problem. For example, there isn't one "best" way to run a homeless shelter or counsel a battered spouse, but there may be "better" ways. The key here is to be able to *measure* as accurately as possible how well a program or idea works. It is important to remember that benchmarking is a *comparative* approach—it helps you decide what works by comparing the outcomes of different programs to see which perform better than the rest. There are several guiding principles you can use to help identify best practices.

- Is there a proven track-record of success?
- Are the results sustainable?
- Can the idea be replicated?
- Is it cost-effective?

## What do you Benchmark?

In a word, you benchmark anything you want to improve or learn to do better. Some organizations benchmark their executive director's salary, comparing it to the salaries of other organizations with similar resources, size, and mission. Some organizations benchmark how much they charge for their services versus others who provide similar services. Some organizations benchmark the number of people they serve compared to similarly-situated organizations in other communities.

An easy rule of thumb is that you can benchmark the three "P's":

- **a Process**, such as screening job applicants or organizing inventory in a food bank;
- **a Policy**, such as salaries or incentive plans; or
- **a Program**, such as welfare-to-work or educational incentives.

To determine what to benchmark, an organization must take a careful look at its own performance. This really involves looking in the mirror and pinching the "fat" of the organization: where is it too sluggish, what does it do well, and so on. In most cases, organizations are interested in benchmarking or improving their programming. This, after all, is their "bread and butter" and is the focus of most of an entity's resources. However, there are often many different facets of an organization that can be improved through shared learning.

## Approaches to Benchmarking

*How* do you benchmark? In other words, how does an organization go about the process of finding best practices and learning from them? Some organizations take a highly academic, or *technical approach*, using computer models, statistics, spreadsheets, and quantitative analysis to determine which practices are the best. Technical benchmarking is often administered by Ph.D.s who measure the impacts of a particular approach as compared to a "control" group over a period of years. Such studies are called "randomized impact studies."

Others take a more piecemeal or *ad hoc approach*. This essentially involves assigning one person the job of reading trade journals and publications, attending conferences, and generally seeking out innovative ideas and model programs on his or her own. Usually the person doing the research uses his or her own judgment as to what is the best idea based upon that person's experience in the field.

The *committee approach* involves bringing in a team of "experts" from outside your organization. These individuals often have policy-making experience and offer credibility as a result of their public reputations. The team usually conducts a variety of interviews and surveys, gathering information through networking and contacts, and then comes to a consensus on which programs are best suited for the organization.

While each organization may decide on its own approach, I recommend a hybrid of the above-mentioned methods called *survey benchmarking*. An organization really wants to emphasize the hard numbers of the technical approach, the flexibility of the individual/ad hoc approach, and the interactive aspect of the committee-style approach.

Survey benchmarking involves putting together a team of individuals, from all levels of the organization. The team must work closely to identify what aspects of the organization should be benchmarked, to define the "measures" used to gauge the organization's performance, to establish the methods for gathering the best practices, and to oversee the process for implementing new ideas.

## Getting Started: 7 Steps to Benchmarking

### 1. *Self-Assessment*

The first thing you must do is determine what your organization wants to benchmark, or improve, about its operations. This requires a detailed self-audit, designed to determine your organization's strengths and weaknesses, problems and proposed solutions, and overall effectiveness in achieving its mission. Interviewing board members, program administrators, and other key personnel in your organization will provide a good starting point. You might also consider asking some of the constituents you serve, some with whom you have been successful, and others with whom you have not, for their assessment of your organization's performance and recommendations for improvement.

### 2. *Measuring Performance*

Once your organization has identified the areas for improvement, you must figure out how to measure what you define as "success" in those areas. This involves some hard thinking, but everything can be measured somehow. Some measurements are easy, like the number of meals served, or the cost per meal.

Other areas are more difficult. For example, measuring success in a counseling program, or whether the pamphlets for an organization's AIDS education program have helped prevent the spread of the disease. In these cases, you must be more creative—maybe using surveys for participants is one way to measure the impact of counseling. Maybe pamphleteering can be measured by the number of phone calls to a hotline advertised in that pamphlet that result in attendance at seminars. While difficult, this part of the process is critical; it calibrates the units of measurement by which to compare your organization's performance to others.

### 3. *Assembling the Team*

Benchmarking is a team-driven activity. Individuals should be chosen because of their role in the organization as well as their skill sets. Interdisciplinary groups are often the most effective. You want a group that has management experience as well as day-to-day contact with the people you serve. You also need some people who can work well with data, some people who are outgoing and comfortable contacting outsiders, and some people who are able to set priorities internally to make sure that new ideas get properly implemented. This usually ends up including accountants, managers, instructors, and researchers, to mention a few. The team should still be manageable in size, usually from 5-8 people, depending on the size of the organization.

### 4. *Data Collection*

The first priority of the team will be to set the scope of its data gathering. Will it look only to local organizations, regional, national or international? A lot of this will depend on the resources of the organization and the time frame it sets for the undertaking. I usually recommend looking beyond one's own locale. On the other extreme, international benchmarking has proven to yield some great ideas, though it can be quite expensive and complex. So each organization must set its own parameters for the search for best practices.

At this stage, the *tools* for investigating best practices must also be determined. How will you do your research on best practices—using associations, the Internet, trade publications, popular media, the library, conferences, hiring experts? All of these are legitimate data collection tools, and your organization must decide what is feasible given your resources and time. Organization of information once you collect it is also critical. Think carefully about how and where to store data on best practices as you gather it.

### 5. *Evaluating Best Practices*

Probably the most difficult stage of the benchmarking process is the evaluation stage. How do you evaluate whether something is a best practice? This comes back to the original four principles (track record, repeatable, sustainable and cost-effective) I identified earlier. Within these guidelines, you must develop a set of measures for comparing the performance of one program to another. As such, it is important to measure the performance of other organizations on the same scale as you measure your own. Otherwise, your team will be left comparing mangos to papaya juice, to use a more tropical example. This will enable you to identify the "performance gap" between your organization and other top performers.

At this stage, you will also have to deal with the question of quality of your data. How do you know that another organization's performance is really as good as it says? There may be "fudging" of numbers, maybe the organization had a particularly charismatic or inspiring leader, or maybe its success was a fluke. All of these variables must be considered on some level when evaluating best practices. While you probably will not arrive at a statistical certainty, you can at least be confident that what you are reading about is in fact true. This requires due diligence.

Often during the evaluation phase, teams will go on site visits as part of the due diligence process. These are useful in two ways. First, interviewing prospective benchmarking partners allow you to take a closer look "under the hood" of the organization you are studying, to see its practices firsthand. Second, site visits build relationships. The implementation phase of benchmarking requires a close working relationship with your benchmarking partners, and meeting them in person is one way to deepen that rapport.

### 6. *Translating Best Practices*

Once you have evaluated and then identified the best practices, your team must focus on how to implement the ideas you have learned. This involves careful analysis of your own organization's resources, structure and organizational culture. Translating or "replicating" a program or technique may be as simple as incorporating a new concept, or as complicated as performing a heart transplant.

In all cases, your team must carefully set the stage for bringing new ideas into the existing organizational framework. Working closely with benchmarking "partners" at the best practice site, both sides will have to be involved in the process, from beginning to end.

### 7. *Continuous Improvement*

Benchmarking is a process that, once put into place, endlessly repeats itself. What's innovative and cutting-edge today may be tomorrow's "bottom line." Making this commitment for the long-haul will result in unprecedented improvements in your organization's morale, performance, and outlook, but it requires constant scouting of new ideas and updating of old ones.

## Common Concerns About Benchmarking

While benchmarking is simply a more sophisticated form of institutional learning, organizations often misconstrue what it means and how it will affect them. Here are a few of the common, instinctive reactions to benchmarking in non-profit organizations:

### "But We're Not A Corporation"

Many protest that benchmarking works only for businesses, that it is a "corporate" tool for management. What's more, some fear the "corporatizing" of the non-profit sector, and believe that emulating business procedures compromises the purity of their organization's mission.

*Actually, non-profits* are *legal corporations that simply don't pay tax. As such, non-profits have similar budgetary demands, management problems, business plans, and performance issues; why not try similar approaches to solving problems? Benchmarking is an "organizational" process more than a "business" process. Therefore, benchmarking works in any organization that has a defined mission, goals, and people working to achieve those goals.*

### "Not Invented Here"

This concern is common with benchmarking in just about any sector. It is often perceived that a solution that is "imported" is second-rate because it was someone else's idea. Moreover, most non-profit managers believe that their services and programs are unique and therefore no one else's solutions "fit" their organization's issues.

*In fact, outside solutions probably won't interface perfectly with your problems. However, in benchmarking, as with shoe inserts, you must always trim around the edges to make a perfect fit before you put it in place. Furthermore, while your organization's services may be unique, odds are that its goals (or issues in achieving those goals) are not. The strength of benchmarking is that it embraces "difference"—learning from the "gap" between what one organization does versus another.*

**"Who Are We To Say What's The 'Best'"**

A common concern among managers is that they know well what works for their own organization but are in no position to judge what works "best" for others. Further, many will respond that "best" is all relative and that no one person can possibly make that determination.

*One of the inherent values in benchmarking is its "secondary" effects on the organization. In fact, non-profit managers* should *be aware of what is going on outside their own organization, and the benchmarking process further develops that awareness. Also, remember that the "best" in best practices applies more to what is "best" for your own organization than finding the "Holy Grail" of solutions. The reason for putting in place a benchmarking team is to form a collective judgment using the best measures that you can to judge performance.*

**"We're Stealing Ideas"**

Some question the morality of benchmarking. The concern here is that one should not be snooping around other people's organizations trying to co-opt their strategies and ideas.

*The bottom line is that benchmarking is done informally every day by non-profit organizations. When you read about a good idea in a trade magazine or hear about an interesting new approach at a conference, these are all examples of considering other people's ideas. The point is that the focus should be on the positive—how can the non-profit sector come together and share ideas or solutions to more aggressively solve society's problems. Besides, benchmarking cannot be done without the cooperation of "partner" organizations, who often are flattered that you find their ideas innovative.*

## Benchmarking Tips

Before beginning the benchmarking process, keep in mind a couple of general tips:

### 1. Think Big, But Not Too Big

To be sure, benchmarking is an ambitious undertaking. To be successful, your organization must enlarge its "world view," embracing new ideas and welcoming outside input. At the same time, you want to be careful not to bite off more than you can chew. Start off with one or two areas to benchmark. Then, when the process gets more familiar, move on to new areas. Many organizations make the mistake of trying to introduce benchmarking throughout the entire organization before trying it out in a couple of key areas. Also, be realistic about the resources your organization can afford to devote to the benchmarking process. This will govern the scope of your efforts—how far and wide you can look for ideas, and how carefully you can measure their effectiveness.

### 2. Prepare, But Don't Overprepare

Careful preparation is essential to successful benchmarking. Internal audits must be conducted, teams must be assembled and resources must be mobilized. This all takes time and energy. However, it does not take an eternity. Take the time to prepare, but don't overprepare. On some level, you need to just jump in and splash around in the process for awhile until you get used to it. It is true that being methodical and organized is essential to a successful benchmarking experience. But sometimes people may be intimidated by new procedures and ideas and instinctively put them off by setting up an endless stream of planning committees, reports, and reviews. Always keep the process on a streamlined, forward-moving schedule.

### 3. Have Fun With It

Benchmarking is serious business, but it can also be a lot of fun. The process allows people to get out of old routines, think outside the box, and even travel. One of the most valuable byproducts of benchmarking is the energy and creativity it produces. Allow your staff the freedom to go with the flow—to seek out and explore new ideas. Encourage discussion and interaction among different levels of the organization around alternative solutions. A process that is enjoyable and engaging will be much more productive, and more well-received than one that is not.

### 4. Don't Search for the Holy Grail

Inexperienced benchmarking teams will often get mired in data collection. While this is a critical phase of the process, it also can be quicksand. The team must realize that there often will not be one clear best practice that will emerge. Don't worry about finding the "best" practice so much as identifying ones that are clearly "better."

### 5. Focus on Implementation

The ultimate pitfall in any benchmarking undertaking is to produce a gleaming, impressive benchmarking report, and then have the recommendations go nowhere. The key to success is in the implementation phase. Involve beneficiaries of the process early and often. Hardwire them into the process by having them design the questionnaires, suggest partners, and review your conclusions.

## Up Close: Jason Saul

Jason Saul is the author of a new book soon to be published by Wilder Publishing Center, *Benchmarking Workbook for Nonprofit Organizations*. The "Introduction to Benchmarking" chapter that appears here is excerpted from Saul's book. Saul currently is the President of the Center for What Works, a New York-based non-profit organization he co-founded in 1994. The mission of the Center is to develop benchmarking techniques for non-profit and government organizations, and to serve as a clearinghouse for best practices in social programming. Before receiving his J.D. from the University of Virginia School of Law, Saul received his Master's in Public Policy from Harvard's Kennedy School of Government. It was at Harvard that his interest in benchmarking was sparked.

"Many of my fellow students at the Kennedy School often discussed the rising anti-government sentiment and the frustration of people with the whole political process," he recalls. "I came to the conclusion that people didn't hate government, per se, but rather they hated the fact that government didn't *work*. I listened to friends at Harvard Business School discuss the concept of benchmarking and how popular it was in corporate America, and I immediately thought of applying such a concept to government."

It wasn't long before Saul recognized its applicability to the voluntary sector. Rena Shulsky, a friend of his who was a venture philanthropist, shared with him her dream of establishing a Center for What Works.

"We originally set out to create a global clearinghouse for best practices in social policy, but soon found that merely collecting policy solutions was only the byproduct of a more valuable underlying process of continuous improvement—benchmarking," he says. "We soon became pioneers in adapting the concept of benchmarking to non-profits and governmental entities."

Saul makes liberal use of the World Wide Web to communicate his ideas and the services provided by the Center for What Works. "At least at the moment, our center has the only public sector/ non-profit benchmarking site on the World Wide Web, and we have seen increasing interest in accessing it," he reports, noting that the address for the Center's site is http://www.whatworks.org. On the site, you can find links to other benchmarking sites and information on public sector and non-profit benchmarking surveys.

"Benchmarking is a tool that knows no boundaries, and there are Internet sites around the world that represent the infinite universe of possible solutions available to those that seek them," Saul continues. Among the Web sites he finds useful for benchmarking are the sites that can be found at http://www.benchmarking.co.uk, http://www.benchnet.com, and http://globalbenchmarking.org.

Saul gives three examples of how benchmarking strategies have helped non-profit organizations improve their quality and performance.

One example is the Museum of Contemporary Art in Chicago (MCA). The MCA regularly benchmarks its fundraising events against those of other major city museums, learning from the sponsorship levels, marketing strategies, and promotional materials of others. A second example is CARE USA—a large international development non-profit organization. CARE used benchmarking to improve the performance of its development and relief services by surveying all of the different projects within the agency, identifying the top performers, and then sharing those lessons learned with other project managers. The final example, STRIVE, a New York-based welfare-to-work initiative, has served as a model for other welfare programs. Program operators from around the country have come to experience STRIVE's unique approach to job training firsthand, taking back fresh ideas to their respective organizations.

While benchmarking is becoming a mainstream organizational improvement strategy, it is not without the potential for problems, including legal concerns. Some potential participants in benchmarking may have questions about exposure to legal liability in sharing information, such as possible violations of copyright or anti-trust laws. Saul seeks to allay those fears and asserts that these concerns should not be an impediment to participation in benchmarking. Simple common sense and a sense of fair play is often enough to alleviate concerns in this area, he says.

"On a conceptual level, benchmarking does not offend copyright protections. Copyright law does not protect ideas or concepts. It is meant only to protect specific expressions and word-for-word plagiarism," he informs. "The only time one must be careful is when using specific linguistic expressions that are unique to an organization, such as copying an organization's mission statement or marketing phrases. As such, the practice of benchmarking is relatively immune to copyright infringement, to the extent that it involves learning from other people's ideas and approaches to solving problems."

As for anti-trust violations, he maintains that reasonable benchmarking practices by businesses competing even directly with each other have so far been accepted as a legal, legitimate business practice. Since non-profit organizations are generally not commercial enterprises, the potential for an anti-trust law violation is negligible.

As perhaps the leading advocate in the United States for benchmarking practices in the non-profit sector, Saul has a vision in which benchmarking will become one of the first strategies of choice by non-profit executives committed to improving their organization's quality and performance. Through speaking to groups, his writing, and through the work of his cutting-edge organization, Saul is making progress each day toward making his vision a reality.

# 5
# Introduction to Outcome-Based Management

***by Gary Grobman and Frederick Richmond***

To improve quality in a larger organization, simply adopting a progressive management philosophy such as TQM is not going to be enough in today's modern competitive business climate. As an organization grows, there are more pressures for accountability, not only internally from a board of directors, but from elected officials, government funders, foundation funders, individual donors and volunteers, and the public. Leaders of large organizations generally do not have the ability to visualize every aspect of their organization's operations and assess what is going on just by looking out their office windows, or by engaging in informal conversations with their staff and clients. The proverbial "one-minute manager" is an ideal construct that is not particularly well-suited to crystallizing the information a CEO needs to make judgments on how to allocate precious resources.

To accomplish the important task of assessing what is really going on within a large organization, most have a Management Information System (MIS) that permits the aggregation of data in a form that can be analyzed by a manager, enabling him or her to see trouble spots and make adjustments in operations and to generate reports required by the government, funders, auditors, and the board of directors.

For many larger non-profits, particularly those that depend on government and foundation grants rather than private donations, the objective of "meeting clients' needs" has become a more formalized process. Times have changed within just the last decade or so. Traditionally, measures of organizational performance for human service organizations were based on a model more appropriate for industrial processes, where raw materials were turned into finished products. In the language of industrial systems analysis, inputs (the raw material) were processed into outputs (the finished product). In adopting an analogous frame of reference to industry, the conventional thinking was that human service agencies took in unserved clients (input), provided services (process), and changed them into served clients (output). In this way of thinking, organizations improved their output by increasing the number of clients served.

An exciting new way of looking at the output of an agency is called outcome-based management (OBM) or "results-oriented accountability" (ROA). Most recently, results-oriented management and accountability (ROMA) has become the buzz-word describing this general tool. All of these terms have similar roots and go back to original work done in the early 1980s by Harry Hatry of the Urban Institute and Reginald Carter who, at the time, worked for the Michigan Department of Social Services. In September 1981, the Urban Institute together with the American Public Welfare Association (now called the American Public Human Services Association), published *Developing Client Outcome Monitoring Systems,* which included both Hatry and Carter among its principal authors. In 1983, Sage Publications, Inc. published Carter's *The Accountable Agency.* These two publications played a prominent role in the development of outcome-based management during the last two decades.

OBM focuses on program outcomes rather than simply quantifying services delivered. Program outcomes can be defined as "benefits or changes for participants during or after their involvement with a program" (from *Measuring Program Outcomes: A Practical Approach, United Way of America).*

For example, an organization dealing with reducing drug abuse may have a stellar record of attracting clients through a flashy outreach program. It may be exemplary in convincing doctors in the community to donate thousands of hours of free services to the program, thereby reducing unit costs per client. It may have few complaints from the clients, who feel the staff are competent and treat them with dignity. An analysis of conventional data might indicate that there is little room for improvement. But, perhaps, no data are collected on whether those treated for drug abuse by the organization are successfully able to become independent, avoid future interactions with the criminal justice system, and rid themselves of the scourge of drug dependence for an extended period of time—all measurable outcomes for a successful substance abuse program. If most of these clients are back on the street and drug dependent, is that organization providing successful treatment even if drug abuse services are being provided? Are funders and taxpayers getting a fair return on their investment?

In the outcome-based management model, the number of clients served is an input. The output is considered to be measurements concerning the change in the condition of the clients after receiving the services. For example, if thousands of clients are served, but the conditions of the clients have not improved, then the outcome is zero, even if the services were provided 100% on time, every client received a satisfactory number of hours of services, and there were no client complaints.

It is no longer indicative of the effectiveness and value of an organization to only collect data on how many clients sought services, how many of these were accepted into the client stream rather than being referred or turned down, how many hours of service were provided, and how much each service cost and was reimbursed. Outcome data together with the above process data are needed to measure the effectiveness and value of an organization.

Major funders of human service agencies are becoming more sophisticated in requiring answers to questions that go beyond the usual data analysis that focuses on costs and the quantity of services being provided. Among them are the U.S. Department of Health and Human Services' Office of Community Services, the U.S. Department of Housing and Urban Development (HUD), and the federal Head Start program. Mainstream charities such as the United Way, the Boys and Girls Clubs of America, and the Girl Scouts are fostering the adoption of outcome-based management in their member agencies.

Increasingly, foundations and government funders seek not only to know if costs are reasonable and clients are receiving services, but whether the provision of these services is actually achieving the broad objectives of the program being funded.

**Government Performance and Results Act**

In addition to a significant change in attitude about the accountability of the private non-profit sector, the passage in 1993 of the *Government Performance and Results Act,* PL 103-62, changed the way federal agencies plan, budget, evaluate, and account for federal spending. The intent of the Act is to improve public confidence in federal agency performance by holding agencies accountable for program results and to improve congressional decision-making. It seeks to accomplish this by clarifying and stating program performance goals, measures, and costs "up front." These changes were implemented beginning in September 1997.

Beginning in March 2000, federal agencies are required to report to the President and Congress about their own performance when compared to goals established for that year, analyze progress toward those goals, and explain any deviations from the goals and impediments encountered during implementation. On the surface, this would appear to affect primarily federal agencies. However, agencies that either directly fund or block grant dollars to the states, who in turn allocate, grant, or contract out those dollars to local government and private non-profit agencies, will similarly have to set up an accountability framework to comply with changes in the federal legislation.

For example, the Administration for Children and Families, specifically its Office of Community Services, funds the Community Services Block Grant (CSBG) to states. The states, in turn, fund Community Action agencies. The Office of Community Services has created an outcome-based management framework entitled ROMA (Results-Oriented Management and Accountability) that is recommended for developing and reporting family, agency, and community outcomes.

Many local government and non-profit agencies that receive CSBG funds have built outcome requirements into their annual reporting systems. Other federal agencies such as the Department of Housing and Urban Development (HUD) are in the process of developing an outcome framework for their community-funded programs.

## Motivations for Outcome Evaluation

All of us have been familiar with the contentious public policy debate that heated up in the '80s and '90s during a time of shrinking government funding and increasing questioning, if not outright cynicism, about the effectiveness of the spending of billions of dollars in federal anti-poverty funds.

The changes in welfare reform laws made by states and the federal government were in a sense a repudiation of the view that federal government money could wipe out hunger, homelessness, and unemployment. Of course, we have no crystal ball to predict what would have happened in the absence of spending these billions of dollars. But in the minds of many hardworking taxpaying voters, there was a prevalent view that the cycle of poverty was not being effectively broken by government funding, and a new strategy was needed to encourage self-sufficiency. Unfortunately, advocates did not have the outcome data to demonstrate that their programs were effective. Funders are increasingly looking beyond their focus of whether services are being delivered in a cost-effective manner, to whether the delivery of the service is successfully accomplishing what was intended. And many forward-thinking organizations are proactively adapting outcome-based management to collect the data they feel are necessary to tell their story to funders, political leaders, advocates, and the public. Why? Because in their own words, it helps them to tell their story.

According to the United Way of America Web site on outcome-based management, the dividends paid by such programs include helping organizations recruit and retain talented staff, increase volunteers, attract new participants, engage collaborators, increase support for innovative efforts, win designation as a model or demonstration site, retain or increase funding, and gain favorable public recognition. The outcomes data can be used by managers to strengthen existing services, target effective services for expansion, identify staff and volunteer training needs, develop and justify budgets, prepare long-range plans, and focus the attention of board members on programmatic issues.

## Implications for Startup

For some organizations, the shift to outcome-based management will have modest cost implications. It may mean more data being collected from clients during intake. It may mean follow-up surveys to see what happens to clients after they have availed themselves of the organization's services. When this information is available, it is of extraordinary value to those who design, administer, and deliver those services.

Most agencies, however, need to know that they will incur short-term startup costs during the first 12-24 months. It is not necessarily that more data are being collected; it is how these data are being integrated into the existing services and physical structure that increases the costs of obtaining outcomes.

Frequently, the outcome does not occur within the agency's scope and, therefore, the agency has to track and follow up on data after the service was delivered in order to identify and measure the outcome. A good example is case management in which case managers often manage an array of programs and services external to their own agency and must track and identify outcomes across a host of other agencies. This has implications for one's own job and begs for the use of computers that in many non-profits are underutilized or are of older technology.

How else does the shift to outcome-based management affect an organization?

First, it can create some perverse incentives. For example, there is more of an incentive for an agency to reject those clients who are judged by intake staff to have little likelihood of having a successful outcome. Even after a client is accepted, the nature and duration of the services provided may change as a result of the pressure on staff to generate statistics compatible with good outcomes. For example, long-term interventions with high cost but a high probability of success may be avoided in lieu of quick-fix, short- and intermediate-term interventions that will generate a swift positive outcome that will show up in the data more quickly.

Second, the mindset of agency staff needs to change about the nature of their work. At present, it is rare to link performance standards to outcomes in non-profit organizations. For example, we know that hitting more than 61 home runs in a major league season is a very rare event, and never happened prior to 1998. Before two players broke the record, the last time the home-run record was challenged and broken was in 1961 with Roger Maris' 61 home runs. Because we understand baseball, we know not to expect batters to hit 80, 100, or 300 home runs in a season even though the average ball player has between 500 and 600 chances (plate appearances) to hit the ball. We also recognize that 66 or 70 home runs is a measure of excellence, the absolute best that can be accomplished. In human services, we can articulate the outcomes, but we do not always know what constitutes success nor can we accept modest results. For example, a large state-funded welfare-to-work program with a permanent job placement rate of 13% for recipients with limited work history and a lack of educational skills is excellent. It may not be readily apparent that 13% here is the equivalent of 70 home runs in one season.

The use of outcome scales reduces the misunderstanding and makes clear realistic expectations for human services outcomes. It also helps separate short, intermediate, and long-term outcomes so that all parties recognize the consequences of limiting success to the quick, short fixes. Where this all comes together is in the use of return-on-investment (ROI) techniques applied to outcomes and outcome scales. In this manner, the agency measures the financial implications of programs and services. If the return on investment is equal to or greater than the cost of the outcome, it minimizes the perverse incentives—since the fiscal mechanism is a common measure of impact and effectiveness.

## Key Questions To Answer and Factors To Consider

Reginald Carter, in the book *The Accountable Agency*, has suggested seven key questions to be answered in building a database model that is responsive to the outcome-based management model. Two additional questions appear here based on the work done by the Positive Outcomes™ organization (Frederick Richmond and Eleanor Hunnemann). The two illustrations of how these nine questions would be answered in the context of a welfare program and an early intervention program are provided as Appendix C.

Mark Friedman, in a May 1997 paper titled *A Guide to Developing and Using Performance Measures in Results-based Budgeting*, suggests that data collection designers consider six factors in developing their performance measurement systems.

1. The most important factor is that the system must have **credibility.** Those viewing and analyzing the data must have some confidence that it is both accurate and relevant. There need to be rules and policies governing data collection methodology to make sure it reflects reality, and it is helpful to have some external or otherwise independent review to assure that credibility is maintained.

2. The system must be **fair.** The system needs to take into account factors that are within the control of the agency and its managers. It should not be used as a "blunt instrument" to punish poor performance, but rather should be a tool to improve performance.

3. The system needs to be **clear.** If the data are provided in a form that is too obscure, too complicated, or uses statistical measures not in the parlance of those who are analyzing them, the system won't be useful and accomplish its purpose.

4. The system needs to be **practical.** The system should be integrated with current data collection methods, so there is not a major increase in the data collection itself and the staff time needed to process it.

5. The system should be **adaptable.** Programs change, policies change, public goals change, and data collection requirements will need to keep pace with these changes.

6. The system needs to be **connected.** The data collection for performance measurement needs to be integrated with other management, budgeting, and accountability systems in order to permit the feedback gained from the performance measurement system to really make a difference in the decision-making of the organization.

Outcome-based management is a better way of managing. It usually takes some time for management, staff, and the board of directors to make the transition and begin understanding the basic concepts. The adoption of OBM usually requires updates to the agency's policies on confidentiality and data management. As staff are required to collect new data, and follow clients beyond the organization's delivery of services, job descriptions may also have to be changed. One unintended consequence of OBM, according to the paper, *What Every Board Member Needs to Know About Outcomes,* is that staff trained in OBM are increasingly being sought out by both government and the non-profit sector, and may find their value increased—requiring pay raises commensurate with their new skills to facilitate retention.

Agencies must also build the data collection infrastructure to handle this change. It may require an increase in computer capability to store and process the data. At least for the moment, there is a lack of user-friendly software compatible with the needs of human service organizations, although some vendors are working on this.

Where do you start? There are several useful publications that provide more details on how to implement outcome-based management in human service organizations.

## United Way's 8-Step Process

The United Way of America's publication *Measuring Program Outcomes: A Practical Approach* suggests an eight-step process for organizations that want to implement OBM. In summary, the process is—

1. Get Ready.
2. Choose the outcomes you want to measure.
3. Specify indicators for your outcomes.
4. Prepare to collect data on your indicators.
5. Try out your outcome measurement system.
6. Analyze and report your findings.
7. Improve your system.
8. Use your findings.

## Conclusion

What makes outcome-based management an easy sell to the human services sector is that it is common sense. What is the point of investing thousands, if not millions, of dollars of an agency's resources if the end result is not accomplishing what is intended by the investment—improving the lives of the agency's clients? Our human service organizations have been established to make people's lives better. When our organizations change their focus to concentrating on doing what it takes to make people's lives better compared to simply providing human services, then it is much more likely that this worthy goal can be accomplished successfully. This is compatible with the values of most in the sector, who often make financial sacrifices to make a difference in the lives of those who need human services.

In cases where the data show that an agency is successfully providing services, but those services are not having the intended effect on the clients, then the agency leadership should be the first to recognize that it is wasteful to keep business as usual. Outcome-based management is a powerful tool to allow organizations to allocate their precious resources to do the most good. If successfully implemented, it can also provide the ammunition to fight the increasing public cynicism about what is often perceived to be a poor return on investment of tax dollars, and provide a competitive edge to organizations that adopt OBM.

## Up Close: Frederick Richmond

Frederick Richmond is the President of the Harrisburg, Pennsylvania-based Center for Applied Management Practices. Founded in January 1998, the Center provides training, on-site technical assistance, and organizational development for community-based organizations, large non-profits, and local and state governments.

Before founding the Center, Richmond spent over a decade as the Director of the Bureau of Research, Evaluation and Analysis, an in-house think tank at the Pennsylvania Department of Public Welfare. Prior to that, he worked at the National Center for Health Services Research, the federal government's think tank for health-based clinical and public health research. It was in his first month with the Department of Public Welfare that he had his first exposure to, and became enchanted with, the outcomes approach to managing human services.

"It was in 1980 when I was asked to fill in for a Pennsylvania state official who was unable to attend a meeting in Washington, DC, hosted by the Urban Institute and the American Public Welfare Association (now known as the American Public Human Services Association)," Richmond recalls. "It was at this meeting that I received my first introduction to the technique of 'Client Outcome Monitoring Procedures for Social Service Agencies,' the term for what we now call results-oriented management, outcome-based management or Results-Oriented Management and Accountability (ROMA)."

It was at this meeting that he met Harry Hatry and Reginald Carter, two of the national leaders in developing outcome-based management.

"We tried to implement Client Outcome Monitoring Procedures in Pennsylvania, but Pennsylvania state government was not as ready as other states, particularly Michigan and Texas, who provided national leadership," he remembers. "People were entrenched in their traditional systems; outcomes were not as important compared to the traditional budget practices of funding based on utilization of services and historical spending patterns."

The department began a modest outcomes effort in 1987, where it was used for external purposes but not for managing within the agency. Richmond left the Department in 1991, and served as a consultant to the PA Department of Community Affairs, which asked him to develop an outcomes curriculum, provide outcomes training to local agencies, and rewrite state program regulations requiring outcomes reporting. How did this agency become enamored with OBM?

"During a state budget appropriations hearing, a state senator asked the Secretary of the Department of Community Affairs what happened to the people who received services funded by the agency? Her reply was to account for the numbers of people who received services and how much was spent," Richmond explains. "The senator again asked what impact these programs made on people's lives, a question that could not be answered by the Secretary."

What was unusual about the episode was not the Secretary's response but that the senator asked the outcome question, Richmond says. "The Secretary's staff eventually tracked me down for advice and from that we began to integrate outcome thinking into the agency, beginning with changes to the regulations governing the Community Services Block Grant and Neighborhood Assistance Programs."

Richmond shares two examples, one positive and one negative, in which the outcomes approach directly affected the survival of a human service agency in Pennsylvania.

"The lack of an outcome-based reporting perspective contributed to a decision by the county commissioners of one Pennsylvania county to terminate services in two family centers because they couldn't justify the expenditure of public dollars where they couldn't see a measurable result," he shares. "For a year, the county commissioners had requested outcome data, but the agency provided little information to justify its programming. The agencies could not demonstrate their impact on families nor generate any data supporting the preventive nature of their program."

As a result, he says, it could not be determined what impact the program may have had in the community. At the end of the fiscal year, the program was not re-funded.

In another county of Pennsylvania, an adult payeeship program (a mental health program where the agency places and maintains clients in the community rather than an institutional setting) was threatened with being de-funded in the middle of a budget cycle.

"The commissioners had planned to cut the program in the middle of the year, and there weren't any data the agency had to counter the decision," Richmond describes. "Fortunately, an agency staff member had attended a workshop on the outcomes approach, took the tools she acquired back to her agency, and used a Return-On-Investment (ROI) model." According to Richmond, her data indicated that 25 clients with previous hospitalizations all stayed out of the hospital for a year, saving $123 in hospital costs for each dollar of program expenditures.

"Not only did the county commissioners decide not to shut the program down, but they re-funded the program for the next fiscal year, as well," Richmond says.

Is this the way all human service agencies will be judged in the future, or is this just one more three-letter acronym fad?

"With privatization, competition, and managed care coming to human services, the basis for funding and decision-making will be performance and, therefore, outcomes," he predicts. "It will become the basis for subcontracting of human services for the foreseeable future."

Policy changes that are driving the welfare reforms of the late 1990s are reducing service dollars and making existing funding more competitive.

"Funders will put those dollars where they will be the most effective," Richmond contends. "Obviously, funders are looking for hard data to support and justify their decisions and, all things being equal, they will fund those that demonstrate that they can produce measurable results and define the product that they produce rather than accepting qualitative, anecdotal indications of a program's value."

What advice does he offer to agencies interested in this new approach to managing programs? Richmond shares seven suggestions.

"First, be willing to accept the disruption that will occur as well as absorb some of the human costs of changing management systems," he implores. "Second, designate someone in the agency, or create a team to take a leadership role. Seek outside funding to hire consultants or other expertise, and make a long-term investment in your management structure," he says. "Third, recognize that adopting this new way of operating will change the way business is conducted throughout the agency—outcome information will be actively used to manage programs and services, not just report client counts and dollars expended.

"Fourth, adopt a proactive approach rather than having it imposed on you later; the costs will be less and the transition will be less painful. If you can't afford it, consider collaboration with similar agencies and pool resources. Fifth, begin with a skeleton or rudimentary system that identifies at least a couple of outcomes per program—and build on this incrementally each year. Sixth, identify a process to collect, analyze, and report outcomes information and develop this into a formal operating system used by all staff in the agency. A manual system should be developed and tested and, when working, be converted into an automated system.

"And last, recognize that these accommodations will change the entire operation of an agency from intake and screening to service provision and outside referrals."

Richmond also has some advice to funders who have joined the outcomes reporting bandwagon.

"Many agencies do not have the in-house capacity or the funds to develop or sustain an outcome-based system on a regular basis," he points out. "It is not an overlay on an existing system but a wholesale change and overhaul of the agency. Funders need to recognize this and provide additional funds for startup and implementation in addition to direct services allocation."

# 6
# Introduction to Large Group Intervention

*by Gary Grobman and Gerald Gorelick*

Large Group Intervention (LGI) is the generic name given to a family of formal change management strategies that involve placing large parts of an organization, or even the entire organization, in simultaneous contact with one another to plan how the organization is going to change. Proponents and users of LGIs believe these methods are particularly well suited for organizations that are seeking to establish a shared vision of their future and to build a road to get there. Some LGI models are designed specifically for organizations that are seeking to change the way their work is done (e.g., through reengineering or business process redesign).

Non-profits successfully employing these LGI methods include numerous communities and cities; school districts, schools, colleges and other educational organizations; foundations; hospitals, hospices, nurse associations, and other healthcare providers; international relief organizations; trade and professional associations; and governmental agencies at the federal, state, and local levels. The LGI experience of a Catholic religious order was the case study for a recent professional journal article.

## LGI Principles

Although many different LGI models have been developed and are in current use, they generally have common origins and are rooted in similar principles. Among these principles are getting the "whole system" into interactive discussion, using a carefully designed mixture of communication elements, using processes designed to make effective use of participants' emotions as well as thoughts, and facilitating effective dialogue while validating differing perspectives.

## Systems Approach

Large Group Interventions are usually staged in a setting away from the workplace, where participants can focus on the objective at hand without the distractions of the normal work environment. Artificial boundaries within organizations, such as functional departments, are routinely and intentionally fractured to facilitate communication and participation. These boundaries often get in the way of addressing important needs of organizations. Strategies such as TQM and BPR, as well as strategic planning itself, demand that each member of the organization think about the needs of the entire organization rather than his or her piece of it. "Democratic," participatory efforts by organizations may facilitate their members to see beyond the borders of their individual organizational niche, and develop the spirit required to make TQM not simply a "program" but a working philosophy.

### LGI Benefits

The general philosophy inherent in planning change is to recognize that there is resistance to change within organizations, and change is more likely to be successfully implemented when people affected can participate in the process, influence the process, and prepare for its consequences. As expressed by one of the architects of the Future Search LGI model, Marvin Weisbord: "People support what they help create." Other practitioners of LGI methods might add, "...and it's a better creation for their involvement."

Much more than a device for overcoming psychological resistance, LGI is an effective approach to substantially improving the planned change and achieving more desirable results for the organization. One dimension of additional benefits is more effective communication about the changes planned. Plans become far less distorted when everyone affected is hearing the same message at the same time, rather than having it communicated through the grapevine, through regular hierarchical channels, or not at all.

Another advantage of LGI is that those affected by the changes can provide invaluable input. It is rare that a few layers of management (or a subset of the full breadth of functions) within an organization can have an adequately detailed grasp of the whole. In most change management strategies, those at the bottom of the hierarchy, who are usually the most aware of the "nuts and bolts" of current reality, are often frozen out of the planning process. Most LGI models bring in a broad base of stakeholders to brainstorm together and to weed out problems and unintended consequences that are often otherwise built into initial designs for change, because they are invisible to the traditionally unrepresentative group of staff involved in planning.

A third advantage of LGI is that it builds a diverse and broad base of support for planned changes. Useful in all cases, this advantage becomes particularly powerful when circumstances alter, planned changes need to be modified, and time is of the essence. Circumstances that otherwise could be expected to derail well-laid plans can be addressed by a robust and already-engaged subset of the organization. Plans are far more open to effective alteration mid-stream when developed via an LGI approach.

LGIs tend to bring together people from various hierarchical levels within the organization, who otherwise may have minimal direct interaction. Many organizational development experts believe that bringing large groups of organizational members together pays an additional dividend, which would not otherwise have been created, of creating positive social linkages among organizational members. Large Group Interventions create a new and different organizational bonding, which increases networks of informal communication within an organization and makes for more robust capabilities.

All of this can occur in a three-day period, significantly curtailing the process time of conventional change management planning.

## Origins of LGI

The origins of LGI are often traced back to the work of Gestalt psychologist Kurt Lewin. During World War II, there was a meat shortage in the United States, leading to rationing. Lewin and Margaret Mead worked with the War Department to find a way to encourage consumers to use unused parts of the cow. Lewin devised an experiment in which an audience was given a seminar about the nutritional value of these animal parts. Half of those participating were sent home after the lecture, and the other half were placed in small groups to discuss what they heard and to decide what they would do. Those who were so inclined were then asked to make a public commitment to try out the recipes using those cuts of beef. The post-test study found that those who made the public commitment were significantly more likely to have actually bought and tried those cuts of beef. Lewin had found a core principle: we are likely to modify our own behavior when we participate in analyzing and solving a problem and are likely to carry out decisions we have helped make.

Lewin's work and theories pointed the way toward a different type of consultation, where rather than sowing seeds of change, the consultant helps a client discover what seeds are already present and whether they can be grown. More than just finding the organization's underlying problem, true diagnosis for Lewin included approaching this task in such a way as to build commitment for action.

His experiments in group dynamics gave rise to the "T-group" of the 1960s and 1970s, and ultimately led to experiments using small group methods in large groups. It was not until the 1990s, however, that large group interventions became a widespread organizational change management strategy. A 1997 book, *Large Group Interventions,* by Barbara Benedict Bunker and Billie T. Alban, published by Jossey-Bass, did in some ways for LGI what Hammer and Champy's *Reengineering the Corporation* did for BPR, creating much broader awareness of, and facilitating organizations' access to, LGI theory and practice.

## Types of Interventions

Bunker and Alban write about eight discrete types of long-term interventions: The Search Conference, Future Search, Real Time Strategic Change, ICA Strategic Planning Process, the Conference Model, Fast Cycle Full Participation Work Design™, Real Time Work Design, and Participative Design. Each management strategy is usually identified with a group of consultants or academics who developed it and earn their livings in the field. Many of the LGI creators write and market publications and step-by-step workbooks, facilitate LGI projects as external consultants, and provide related services, such as conducting educational seminars for organization consultants and others who want to learn more about LGI.

## Effectiveness of LGI

Change management strategies, such as those described in previous chapters, have had a checkered record of success. Management is continually searching for a single elixir or magic potion that will result in improved performance. Rarely has a prepackaged new management system, such as BPR or TQM, lived up to its promises. Some of this may be attributed to faulty implementation. And some can be attributed to workers who have not bought into the changes.

Permitting workers affected by planning to participate in the planning process is one strategy to erode this resistance to organizational change, in addition to generating fresh ideas from people who have expertise as a result of doing their job every day. They may have shied away from making valid, responsible suggestions not only because "no one ever asked us" but because they may feel that their views are not important, or that management does not have an interest in listening to them.

There is not very much empirical information about the success of large group interventions, and most of what we know today is anecdotal. It can be quite costly to shut down an organization for several days for an organizational retreat, and the out-of-pocket costs for consultants, meeting room space, food, materials, and keeping the organization functional while all of this is going on can be prohibitive for many non-profit organizations. Yet the basic theory of large group intervention, that changing an organization through top-down edict often fails because of resistance at the lower levels, may justify this change management strategy. What appears to consume a large amount of resources may in fact be a tremendous time and cost saver when all the false starts, multiple sessions, and cascading communications of an alternative approach are tallied up.

### Theoretical Underpinnings/Resistance to Change

An important element in introducing change management techniques is recognizing that humans are resistant to change. First, workers feel that their jobs are threatened. BPR, for example, is identified with massive downsizing and dislocation. Even if employment is not at risk, changing the working conditions, responsibilities, or perceptions alone can appear threatening and engender resistance.

Second, workers reach a comfort level in performing their jobs, and changes in how work is performed suggest that they may have to learn new job skills. For some, this is a positive aspect, but for others, it increases worker insecurity. There is a fear of the unknown.

## Various Models

A representative sample of the more popular LGIs is described below:

### *1. The Search Conference*

The Search Conference was designed by Englishman Fred Emory and Australian Eric Trist. It evolved out of a consulting job to help plan the future of an aeronautical engineering company, which had recently fused from two companies. Conferences are comprised of 30-60 people, selected from within an organization as the key movers and shakers—the experts, those with the most influence, those who will be implementing change, and the general organizational leadership. At least two days are allocated to the conference.

The first task of the conference is to perform an environmental scan in which, through a brainstorming session, attendees make a list of significant external changes affecting the organization within the last 5-7 years. They then break up into small groups and analyze how these changes affect the organization and predict both likely and desirable futures of the organization. The second step is for attendees to make a list of organization milestones and other important developments since they joined the organization, with the longer-tenured employees speaking first.

Third, a list is made (by brainstorming) of what features in the organization need to be changed. Fourth, small-group discussions, working in parallel, focus on the elements that would comprise an ideal organization in the future. Fifth, the conference engages in action planning. Strategic goals are agreed upon, and small groups are convened for each goal to develop the steps to accomplish each of those goals, including a timetable. Finally, a plan is developed for implementation, which often utilizes the democratic, self-managing structures created at the conference rather than the hierarchical, bureaucratic structure of the organization. This intervention is used mostly to improve management in the workplace and empower workers.

### *2. Future Search Conference*

The Future Search Conference evolved out of the work of Marvin Weisbord and Sandra Janoff, and is detailed in several books authored or co-authored by one or both of them, including *Productive Workplaces* (1987), *Discovering Common Ground* (1992) and *Future Search* (1995). It typically brings into the same room all of the people of the organization with a stake in its success and may involve as many as 100 participants (although 65-80 is the typical size). Included are those who may not be members of the organization but are important external stakeholders, such as customers and suppliers.

The 16-hour conference conducted over three days focuses on planning for the future and includes highly structured participatory interaction. Consultants who facilitate these conferences guide discussion to look at the work done by the organization and its goals in the context of the outside environment, and focus on reaching a consensus on what constitutes "common ground" as a basis for building the desired future. Areas in which consensus cannot be reached within a reasonable period of time are acknowledged but do not become a focus of the group's work. Much of the work of the conference is done by 8-member subgroups that manage themselves.

The conference does not bring in outside experts but depends on the expertise of the participants themselves. Planning meetings are held prior to the conference to set the tone and direction, and provide the context for building the work product, which is the development of action plans. During the conference, activities include examining the organization's relevant past, looking at the present in terms of the situation and the problems facing the organization and external trends affecting it, and identifying priorities. Participants develop stronger ownership of the status quo and responsibility for the future by identifying what they are proud of, or sorry about, with respect to the main problem identified as the focus of the conference; develop a vision for the "ideal" future; identify common themes; and develop "first step" action plans with explicit accountabilities by using brainstorming and breaking up into small planning groups.

Followup meetings are held to maintain participants' views of the whole system and to check on progress. This intervention is used mostly to facilitate collaborative action toward reaching a goal.

### 3. *Real Time Strategic Change*

The Real Time Strategic Change™ method of LGI was pioneered by Kathleen Dannemiller, Robert Jacobs, and several other consultants who perfected the technique at Ford Motor Company. RTSC (now called Whole Scale Change™ by Dannemiller's firm), which usually takes place over a three-day period, involves an entire organization from top to bottom in a strategic planning process. Whole Scale™ conferences typically involve 300-900 participants, but through the use of technology and sophisticated, comprehensive logistical planning, some Whole Scale™ interventions have involved thousands of people at a time. A first step in Whole Scale™ is for organizational leadership to agree among themselves how much power they're willing to relinquish to the participants.

Leadership is called upon to agree upon initial constraints on the degree to which they are willing to permit participants to influence the outcome. However, the general thrust is to allow people who are affected by the strategic planning to have a say in putting the plan together. RTSC includes an environmental scan so participants can understand the current situation and the changing nature of the environment. They often hear the perspectives of outside experts, including clients and customers. Small-group discussions involve participants selected from a wide range of suborganizations, so each participant hears various perspectives. When RTSC is successful, it is often the result of management positively responding to the suggestions made at the conference by participants, who then feel empowered.

The structure of the conference is based on a model of organizational change that suggests that change will only occur when resistance to change is overcome, and that three factors—dissatisfaction (a decrease in the comfort level people have with the organization), vision (a shared sense of overall direction of the organization), and the ability to move the organization in the direction of positive change (known as "first steps")— are large enough.

### Relative Strengths/Weaknesses

Large Group Intervention techniques have also been created to make BPR participatory throughout the organization. LGI is used to foster communication among all workers relating to plans to make any major changes in vision, work processes, organizational structure, and human resources issues. Details about some of the techniques can be found in the Bunker and Alban book, and new methods are being developed and refined constantly. A family of LGIs is devoted to improving workplace design and business processes. Among them are The Conference Model™, Fast Cycle Full Participation Work Design, Real Time Work Design, and Participative Design. The Conference Model™, designed by Dick and Emily Axelrod, uses five 2-3 day conferences over a five-month period to compress the time that conventional reengineering processes take, and is much more participatory than BPR. Fast Cycle Full Participation Work Design™ is a method attributed to Dr. William Pasmore of Case Western Reserve University. It is used to increase the velocity of changes made in the socio-technical aspects of organizations, and involves analyzing how an organization's social resources (the skills of its workers, knowledge and experience, communication networks) are consonant with its technical resources (how the work actually gets done).

## Tips for Beginning a Large Group Intervention

Various LGI experts point to different factors they deem critical to the success of an intervention, but many of these differences appear to be matters of emphasis rather than real disagreements. Here, then, are some of the key considerations before deciding to take up LGI within a particular organization:

1. Take the time and care to achieve clarity of purpose: what does the organization want to be different as a result of this undertaking? Invest a lot of conversation to get the issue framed well and stated well.

2. Be willing to step into some anxiety and unknown waters in order to achieve something extraordinary.

3. Involve the whole system, or at least a critical mass that is truly representative of the whole. Use a steering group that cuts a diagonal slice through all the organization's layers and across all its functions.

4. Create conditions for effective dialogue among people with different perspectives. Use experienced resources to guide the design and to facilitate the large-group events. Interactive meetings of 80-100 people (or more) are not the place for untrained facilitators.

## Up Close: Gerald Gorelick

Gerald Gorelick is President and founder of Gerald Gorelick & Associates, Inc., a Harrisburg-based consulting firm focusing on conducting large group interventions and other organizational development services for small- and mid-sized businesses, not-for-profit organizations, and governmental units. He started the company after 21 years of senior management experience with HMOs, insurers, hospital and health centers, and a data processing/service company. A student of organizational effectiveness throughout his management career, he was an agent for transformational change in several of the organizations he worked for, introducing quality circles, TQM and BPR, and other methods for producing significantly better operating results. He received formal training in Future Search by its originators, and in Whole Scale Change™ by Kathleen Dannemiller and her associates.

"I've personally been part of both Future Search and Whole Scale™ events," Gorelick relates. He points out that Future Search is the LGI model of choice for organizations that want to create a different future for themselves, a future that reflects the best thinking of the whole range of their stakeholders (management, staff, board members, clients, funders, volunteers, and so on) and that enjoys these stakeholders' active support and involvement. "The entry point may have been desire for a compelling strategic plan, a need for building common ground or community across diverse interests, or the apparent need to build new partnerships," he says. "I've seen Whole Scale™ used to redefine the respective roles of human resources and management in a large governmental agency and to redesign a core business process for another agency."

In his experience, Whole Scale™ or Real Time Strategic Change can accommodate very large groups of participants in a single event, compared to Future Search.

"I've seen Whole Scale™ or Real Time Strategic Change with as many as 400 participants and I know of successful engagements with several thousand," he says. "Future Search is a very well-crafted model but it is limited to perhaps 50-100 participants—but it is highly reliable in delivering on its promises of defining common ground, creating a shared picture of an organization's desired future, and initiating action steps that cut across established boundaries."

Marv Weisbord, who together with Sandra Janoff designed the Future Search model, has been a consultant and teacher to Gorelick over many years and has shared limitations of the technique.

"Weisbord and Janoff have taught me that Future Search conferences do not allow you to make up for weak leadership, transform a bureaucratic culture in 48 hours, teach people how to learn, or change the dynamic interactions of any intact group in 48 hours," Gorelick points out. "What this strategy does permit you to do is speed up discovery, learning, and action planning enormously; build better relationships across critical boundaries, such as with boards of directors; and stimulate voluntary actions that need to happen but cannot be legislated, planned, led, or even envisioned in advance. No one knows what's really needed, what others want, or what's desirable or practical until they discover it together in the conference.

"Initiating a Large Group Intervention strategy can often be stressful for organizations," he contends. "Leadership typically feels a combination of excitement and anxiety about these processes. This is to be expected, since it entails stepping out into the unknown to a certain extent, and charting new territory for the organization in a more 'public' setting than usual," Gorelick maintains. "A key component of this type of intervention is for me to spend time early on with management so that they understand what this type of intervention entails for them and for the rest of the organization, and so that I can make my own assessment of their readiness."

For those without personal, firsthand experience attesting to the success of LGIs, there is an appropriate amount of skepticism around the proposition that "real work" can get accomplished interactively in a room of 60 or 600 people. Experienced consultants use techniques to allay these concerns.

"Concerns around potential chaos, dominating and/or silenced voices, and falling into 'groupthink' are legitimate but very effectively addressed in the LGI model designs I've been involved in," claims Gorelick. "It can be—and perhaps should be—a roller coaster as the event unfolds. But by its end, people are surprised at how far they've come individually and collectively," he perceives. "There's a point in every successfully planned and executed event, typically not occurring until the last day, where the group, and the organization, makes a turn," he observes. "Those who attend coalesce around a commonly held vision, fueled by a legitimate dissatisfaction with the status quo and guided by the collective creation of a set of action steps with accountabilities owned, and the energy is at a level that ensures that desired differences will take hold."

Gorelick says that new relationships are forged that make for a far-more-robust support net for the planned transformations than any traditional type of planning process.

What advice does he have for the non-profit executive thinking about implementing a Large Group Intervention?

"Find someone who has experience designing and running them, and have an exploratory conversation," Gorelick recommends. "A manager who finds him or herself thinking 'there's got to be a better way' and who has an inclination to try something that will tap the hearts and minds of more than the usual people involved, would be well served to look into these methods, but it is not something to be undertaken without experienced assistance."

# 7
# Introduction to Chaos Theory

People have been managing formal organizations for several thousand years, beginning with armies, religious institutions, and secular government. Yet despite the concerted efforts of hundreds of academics, practitioners, and forward-thinking scientists, futurists, and philosophers, there appear to be no constant, simple, applicable rules for managers to follow that are universal. The science of management has come a long way in just 20 years, but compared to what we know about the physical world, the science of managing people is still in its infancy.

And it may always be so. People are so individualistic, interactions between people are so unpredictable, and so many variables appear to affect what occurs in an organization that outcomes do not appear to be predictable, given the initial starting conditions and information about events that change those conditions. That is why many people consider managing organizations more art than science and why one of the prevailing models of decision-making in organizations is Charles Lindblom's concept of "The 'Science' of Muddling Through," the title of a classic paper he wrote in 1959 that suggested that there are limits to rational decision-making by managers faced with too many competing values, too many changing variables, and only so much gray matter in the cerebral cortex available to process it.

Science *can* tell us a lot about management, however. The work of management thinkers, such as Herbert Simon, Max Weber, Peter Drucker, and Robert Golembiewski, have provided managers with some general principles about management.

For centuries, ideas about managing people have paralleled ideas about the nature of the physical world. The science of chaos theory is providing managers with a new perspective on how to manage their organizations and to consider the effect of even the smallest changes they make.

Every experienced manager has at some time experienced a small glitch that somehow gets magnified and causes a major catastrophe. An employee gets sick, a major project goes uncompleted as a result, and dire consequences befall the organization. Or a freak storm requires the cancellation of a board meeting and, as a result, one particularly argumentative, hostile board member shows up at the rescheduled meeting and changes the course of the organization forever. There is an aphorism that appears in a somewhat edited form in Benjamin Franklin's 1735 edition of *Poor Richard's Almanac* that expresses this thought:

> *"For want of a nail, the shoe was lost;*
> *For want of a shoe, the horse was lost;*
> *For want of a horse, the rider was lost;*
> *For want of a rider, the battle was lost;*
> *For want of a battle, the kingdom was lost!"*

Or, conversely, a chance meeting on the street results in a collaboration that transforms the organization in a positive way. Or, perhaps, you were planning to spend the day having a picnic, but it started to pour, and you rushed into the local mall, found this book in your local bookstore and decided to buy it and have your mind opened up to new ideas, implementing TQM and BPR simultaneously in your organization.

Chaos theory is concerned with the performance of dynamic, non-linear systems. The word "chaos" in this context is a misnomer. The implication of the theory is that seemingly random behavior in nature shows structure and pattern.

A linear system is one that reacts to an outside stimulus in a proportional way. Non-linear systems are those that react to even small outside stimuli in a large, disproportionate way, and may even react to a small change in a more pronounced way than to a large change. Systems that exhibit chaotic behavior show output that appears random and disorderly, but yet is random and disorderly within clearly denoted boundaries. When a manager comes home from the office and writes down what occurred during the day, typically the day was filled with putting out fires, unanticipated distractions, and wildly diverging demands for the manager's time. Yet the manager is able to return to the office day after day and experience much of the same thing, even if the "thing" is constantly changing.

## Roots of Chaos Theory

Chaos theory has its roots in modern physics, chemistry, and biology. Quantum mechanics and relativity theory have required much of classical physics to be revised, and to be applicable only under certain conditions. For many years, the flight of electrons around an atomic nucleus was thought to resemble the apparent clockwork stability of planets orbiting the solar system. We know now that this is not the case; randomness and uncertainty seem to permeate *both* the microcosm and the macrocosm. In chemistry, complex chemical compounds demonstrate nonlinearity when subjected to internal and external events, but they often transform as a result of breaking apart by forming new and even more complex compounds (as, for example, noted in the discoveries of Hya Prigogine, the 1977 Nobel Laureate in chemistry).

And in biology, the science of evolution, once thought to be the result of slow, steady, incremental changes in genetic material, has had to be modified to account for apparently quantum leaps in the complexity of new species within a relatively short time frame.

Chaos theory is a *new* science that accounts for the fact that very small changes in initial conditions of a system can lead to very divergent outcomes. This theory is completely revolutionizing the physical sciences, and recently has gained credence as having important ramifications to management science as well. Organizations are viewed now as non-linear systems. Some days are stable and calm, and some days are filled with random, unpredictable "turbulence" that results in events that completely change the organization in a way that, unlike systems in an orderly, mechanistic, deterministic model, are not reversible.

The theory's modern origins date back to 1960 when a meteorologist, Edward Lorentz, was using a computer to make weather predictions. He set up a computer model based on 12 equations. Wanting to save some time and paper while running the program a second time, he rounded off a single data point from .506127 to .506. He expected to get results approximately equal to the first outcome, but instead, found a completely unexpected, counterintuitive, and massive divergence from the first outcome.

Adherents of chaos theory have labeled this phenomenon the "butterfly effect." Half in jest and half seriously, it refers to a hypothetical situation in which a butterfly in Tokyo happens to flap its wings creating barely measurable air turbulence, and as a direct result from a cascade of events, a storm occurs in New York that otherwise would not have. A more precise mathematical term for the butterfly effect is for a system to demonstrate a "sensitive dependence to initial conditions."

There are many common phenomena in nature that seem to verify the tenets of chaos theory. Every snowflake is unique, a result of the fact that minute changes in humidity, air pressure, and wind have large effects on the formation of the crystal that creates each flake. Each person's fingerprint is unique. The structure of clouds, tree branches, and coastlines show the phenomenon of scaling, in which the micro structure has the same general appearance as the macro structure. The stock market is considered to display chaotic behavior, in that it is possible to predict trends but not data points day to day.

Chaos theory looks at what appear to be random data and randomly patterned physical structures, and surprisingly finds patterns that otherwise might not be readily discernible. For example, making a graph of Lorenz's three equation model for a simple system that also displays sensitivity to initial conditions, creates the equations that precisely describe a water wheel. The equations, when graphed, never repeat, are not periodic, and appear to be random, except for the fact that they form a double spiral curve that never repeats, and looks like a butterfly on the page. The graph is called a Lorenz attractor, and management theorists who apply chaos theory, such as L. Douglas Kiel, encourage managers to find attractors for their work processes and draw conclusions from looking at these graphs.

Looking at the output of an organization, some days might show excellent productivity and other days minimal productivity. Each day might appear to be unique, and random. Yet chaos theory provides tools to find the structure of even apparently random output of an organization, and use that structure to extract useful information. Just as Lorenz graphed attractors to see the pattern of random data, non-profit organization managers can do the same.

An attractor is a graph of output for a variable over time. It is called an attractor because while any data point seems random, looking at the graph suggests that these points are "attracted" to a region on the graph. The attractor shows how fast or slow the data points are changing compared to the previous data points; that is, the incremental difference in their value. Rather than being plotted as a line graph, the data points are graphed on a Cartesian graph. This Cartesian graph consists of four quadrants. If the value of each data point is continuing to increase, for example, most of the points on the graph will be in the upper right quadrant. A chaotic attractor in which the data oscillates randomly throughout its attractor boundary is graphed as the butterfly-shaped figure first shown by Lorenz. You can see pictures of these attractors by visiting some of the Web sites listed in the *Internet Resources* section of this book.

Chaos theory upholds that even in inorganic systems, it is impossible to predict outcomes with any certainty because of the inability to make small enough measurements to counter the wildly changing outcomes that result from these small differences in initial conditions. For example, even if computer models improved enough and valid data could be collected from points in the atmosphere at one-foot intervals in three dimensions over the entire globe, long-term weather forecasting would still be impossible according to chaos theory.

Every student in statistics learns about the bell curve, and about the law of large numbers, which essentially states that everything eventually evens out given enough time. (This law actually states: "If the number of times an experiment is repeated is increased, the ratio of the number of successful outcomes to the number of trials will tend to approach the theoretical probability of the outcome for an individual event.") For example, flip a fair coin four times and it would not be unusual for heads to occur more or less than half. But flip a coin a billion times and a graph showing the amount of outcomes will always approach 50% heads and 50% tails.

Chaos theory directly contradicts this frame of reference, suggesting that outcomes do not necessarily even out over time, and that outliers on the bell curve (that is, events or data points that vary greatly from the average) often disrupt the equilibrium of systems enough to completely change them into new systems.

Those who watched the popular film *Jurassic Park* heard actor Jeff Goldblum explain chaos theory for the first time in the popular media. Our very existence as a species may well be the result of chaos theory at work. Sixty-five million years ago, an asteroid may have hit the earth and completely wiped out the dominant species on the planet, the dinosaur. Had this highly improbable, chance event not occurred, humans would not have evolved into the apparently dominant species.

## Management and Chaos Theory

What does this say about management? One oft-quoted piece of advice for those who run organizations is "Don't sweat the small stuff." Chaos theory suggests that you *should* sweat the small stuff.

Management science and its physical science counterparts were on a parallel course for many years. Taylorism in management was a mirror image of Newtonian physics—a mechanistic, reductionist viewpoint in which the component parts of a system could be broken down and analyzed, and adjustments could be made. And the outcome would reflect a linear relationship to the input. For example, increasing the 10-worker production line by one worker would, approximately, increase production by 10%. But chaos theory predicts that even in complex systems that are inorganic (such as weather), it is impossible to predict outcomes based on a small change in input. And in organic systems, such as organizations, there is even greater likelihood that small interactions result in disproportionate effects.

"Efforts to make the workplace more productive, such as diversity training or organizational development techniques to promote communication, can be viewed as efforts to change that employees' use in the workplace," writes Kiel in the 1994 book *Managing Chaos and Complexity in Government*. "These changes, however, can generate surprises for management. The nature of non-linear interactions suggests that even such positive workplace interventions may bring on a new set of unintended outcomes."

The fact is that the reductionist view of reality may no longer apply with validity. Everything is connected to everything else. Making a small change here affects the entire system, and changing the system affects connected systems.

Organizations are, of course, organic. The variables involved in even a small group of people are infinite. A good illustration of this point is a baseball game. Virtually everything about this game is controlled. The field is always the same size. The pitcher's mound is exactly the same distance away. The ball is the same size and weighs the same. The lineups of the players may be the same. The rules don't change. So why is it that every game you see is totally different (that is what makes baseball so interesting, of course) even if the conditions are purposely duplicated by having the same lineups, same pitcher, same field, same rules, and so on?

The reason is that chaos theory is at work. Everything may look the same. But the pitcher may have had toast with his coffee in the morning instead of eggs. A fan may have yelled something distracting to the batter. The umpire may blink at an inopportune time. A runner may have a toenail brushing against his shoe in a way that makes him a split second slower getting to first, causing an out rather than a hit. To the discerning fan, every game has a different outcome. And it is not unusual to see something strange and memorable at a game even after watching thousands of them, and perhaps even see something that has never happened before.

And this description is for a system in which the conditions are highly controlled compared to that of a typical organization office environment where people get sick, telephone calls disrupt, weather changes moods, and people interact in a myriad of unpredictable ways.

## Change in Organizations

Erich Jantsch, in a 1980 book, *The Self-Organizing Universe: Scientific and Human Implications of the Emerging Paradigm of Evolution*, identified three stages of looking at change—deterministic change, equilibrium-based change, and dissipative or transformational change. Management theorists have looked at his model and tried to apply them to organizational theory.

Deterministic change is related to the Newton model of physics that dominated science (and management as well) until the 20th century. Apply a force to an object after knowing the initial mass and velocity, and you can predict where that object will be at any future point. A manager knowing that a worker produced 10 widgets on the average could produce an additional

10 widgets by simply hiring one worker. Under this model, a grand theory of management would be possible if one simply had enough information, and could then apply this information to any organization, and essentially could expect the same outcome after doing so. Under this model, management's job was to control workers, and tinker here and there with policies, so output would increase.

A second stage of thinking in the Jantsch model is equilibrium-based change. This model had its roots in biological systems rather than physical systems. It is an "organic" model in that unlike the deterministic system, the equilibrium system adapts to, or resists, the external stimulus in order to maintain a balance or equilibrium. It does so to avoid instability, large variation, and disorder. Organizations under this model resist change, and change can be accomplished only by small, incremental steps. For example, the father of scientific management, Frederick Taylor, identified a phenomenon called "soldiering," in which workers informally agree to maintain a minimal, acceptable level of output among themselves so as to avoid group discord.

The third stage in the model is transformational change. It is this stage that is consistent with chaos theory's prediction that random disorder and instability act to increase the possibility for transformation that makes radical, dramatic changes in an organization. Reengineering is a strategy that seeks to take advantage of this model. Managers don't have enough information to predict what will happen from their management interventions, and thus cannot seek to control their workers. What managers can do is to liberate their workers to control themselves, and provide them with the tools and technology they need to manage themselves.

How should the manager deal with what chaos theory teaches?

First, as pointed out by management thinkers well before chaos theory became in vogue, communication is a key to organizational survival rather than control and rational efficiency. Communication permits the organization's members to adapt quickly to changing conditions. Even the most astute manager simply doesn't have enough information to control all staff efficiently (and even if all of the information were available, it would be of such quantity to militate against being able to rationally process it) compared to giving staff authority to organize and control themselves to adjust to the turbulence of changing conditions.

Second, managers need to overcome their bias in favor of mechanistic, linear relationships among their human resources and other inputs and see that non-linear relationships are more likely to describe how people and other resources interact with each other. It means that it is almost impossible to predict the future of an organization because that future is affected by unexpected events. For example, the loss of a single employee in a large organization may have devastating effects on productivity well beyond the value-added contribution of that worker. Increased communication may act to limit the disproportionate deleterious effects of small changes.

Third, recognizing that small changes in processes can have disproportionate overall effects, managers should be looking for these opportunities that some academics have called "lever points" or "leverage." TQM is one such possible source of leverage. Making a small, incremental change in some process might well provide the straw that breaks the camel's back and provides a quantum improvement in a process. Or, as one writer pointed out, it is possible that someone adopting statistical process control may be graphing data points and finds a point outside of the upper control limit that just happened at random. Looking at what caused that data point, a change in the process may be suggested that reengineers the process.

Of course, you could make the argument that as a result of finding that random point, a process that was actually in control and working quite well may have been reengineered, causing harm just as easily as benefit. But that is what chaos theory predicts—a small change results in disproportionate results, without a bias as to whether the change is positive or negative to the system. Managers need to be aware of this, plan for it, and perhaps even embrace it.

While it is easy to look at chaos theory in a negative light from the perspective of managers who want stability in their organizations, chaos theory can provide positive motivation for change as well. It is often the "not average" events that occur that permit creative managers to reshape and reengineer their organizations so that they can adapt to changing conditions. Good managers don't just want to see their organizations survive. They should strive to enhance their organization's ability to meet the needs of society. Chaos theory provides the unexpected events that permit creative managers to evolve their organizations, and find opportunities that would not otherwise present themselves.

Chaos theory is still developing as a science, and applications of this new frame of reference are being found almost universally in every field of human endeavor. As managers take steps to change their organizations to improve quality and performance, they should be aware of what chaos theory says about even small, incremental interventions.

## Up Close: Dr. Douglas Kiel

Dr. Douglas Kiel, the author of *Managing Chaos and Complexity in Government*, is the director of the Master of Public Affairs program for the University of Texas at Dallas. An associate professor of government/politics and political economy, Dr. Kiel also serves as the campus's internal total quality management consultant. He has written extensively on chaos theory and its applications to organizations, and believes that non-profit organizations should pay more attention to the lessons that chaos theory teaches, particularly if they are considering introducing a change management strategy.

"Chaos theory can tell us a lot about the challenges of implementing new management strategies such as TQM and reengineering," he asserts. "The obvious danger is that any change effort creates new uncertainties and the potential for chaos."

However, even chaos bounces around within defined parameters, he observes.

"These parameters represent the 'order in chaos.' What managers need to know is what the parameters are that they can expect, or perhaps tolerate, during change efforts," he relates. "If we had a better understanding of the parameters that our work systems function in we might better appreciate what will be lost and gained during change efforts," he adds. "We might begin to realize that our systems are pretty chaotic already and thus see that these new approaches might actually help us settle things down and make managing easier."

Despite a popular notion that many of the effects of chaos theory at work are negative and tend to wreak havoc in organizations, Kiel views chaos theory as a positive weapon in the manager's arsenal that he or she can proactively harness to improve his or her organization's quality and performance.

"Chaos theory teaches us that instability, disorder, and uncertainty can be of real value to managers and organizations," Kiel says. "The dominant management model has a strong control orientation that tries to avoid instability, disorder, and uncertainty. Yet, how many practicing managers think they can really avoid the chaos of organizational life? When we begin to recognize that instability, disorder, and even a little chaos can lead to new opportunities to create new forms of organization and management, we may find that we can develop new methods for dealing with the turbulence of the current non-profit environment."

Kiel feels that inducing dynamic instability is a positive force to keep an organization "on its toes" to sustain its overall viability. He also points out that chaos theory also gives us new insight about how we view strategic planning.

"It seems that we thought we could implement and achieve strategic goals with some kind of engineering accuracy," he observes. "But the reality of managing is that there may be multiple pathways to achieving our strategic goals." Non-profit organizations are increasingly turning to these formal planning efforts, but often find unpredicted events thwarting their efforts. He offers two examples of "butterflies" that changed non-profit organizations, one apparently negative and one positive, and which even the most professional strategic planning effort would not have taken into account.

The first example is the infuriating scandal of the United Way of America in 1992, where ethical lapses by its CEO had serious repercussions not only for the national association and its innocent local affiliates, but for the entire voluntary sector. But Kiel also sees the silver lining of this episode. "Didn't this incident force the new leadership to really rethink its strategies and tactics? Can't we see this example of disorder as an opportunity for an organization to really reconsider what it is trying to accomplish?"

His second example is the story of the American Paralysis Association.

"Consider how Christopher Reeve became the lead spokesperson for this important organization," he points out. "It took just one very quick and small chance event when riding his horse that totally changed his life. This single, small butterfly of an event provided the American Paralysis Association with a respected, articulate, and highly visible spokesperson. In this case, Mr. Reeve's tragedy can be seen as an organizational butterfly. Such butterflies need not result from tragedy, but most importantly, such stories remind us that small events can have amplifying effects."

What can non-profit managers learn from all of this?

"Chaos theory has much to offer non-profit managers if we are willing to re-examine our views of change. Usually we think of change efforts as proportionate with the amount of change we hope to achieve," he says. "Chaos theory tells us, however, that we may be able to identify leverage points, or butterflies if you will, in organizations and with our employees that allow relatively small efforts to amplify change. The challenge is to look deeply into our organizational and work structures for those points," he implores.

"We need to examine the deepest held beliefs and commitments to processes that people hold and consider what changing these values might do," he summarizes. "We also need to be more thoughtful about how our organizations move in time. For example, we need to be thinking if there is a point in time where our people may be more responsive to such leverage relative to other points in time."

The challenges of introducing change management into an organization are perplexing enough, but managers willing to take the risks of doing so should consider the confounding effects predicted by chaos theory. Kiel's research and writing is on the cutting edge of this promising new science, which has lessons for even the most experienced non-profit organization manager.

# 8
# The Role of Boards in Change Management

The members of a board of directors of a non-profit are the "owners" of an organization. As the chief governing councils, their role in deciding to implement TQM, or any other change management strategy, and assuring that this philosophy is adopted from top to bottom, can be pivotal in TQM success or failure. Power between board and staff develops with organizational culture—the ideology, values, rituals, system of rewards and punishments, and accepted norms of behaviors that make each organization's style unique.

Board members and board chairs serve for set terms. The balance of power between the CEO and the board oscillates constantly in a non-profit organization, depending on many factors, such as the motivation, time constraints, geographical accessibility, management style of the board/board chairman and the consolidation of power, respect, philosophy, type of organization, and culture of the organization.

Historically, people considered serving on a non-profit board to be an honor rather than a job with fiduciary responsibility. Until recently, there were few, if any, guides to participating on a non-profit board. The formation of organizations that provide publications, workshops, and general information, such as the National Center for Non-Profit Boards, the Association of Governing Boards, Independent Sector, and the National Council of Nonprofit Associations (and its state-wide affiliates), is a comparatively contemporary development. Board members rarely received any training or even an orientation. For many organizations, governance was either performed *de facto* by the paid staff with the board serving as a rubber stamp or, at best, an oligarchic management of a few volunteers.

This has changed for many reasons. First, there are new legal requirements with respect to financial accountability. Those who serve on boards are, more and more, asking for information, and refusing to rubber-stamp decisions. They can be financially liable in some cases of particularly egregious examples of mismanagement. Second, highly publicized scandals have rocked the non-profit world, as mentioned earlier. Third, non-profit management is becoming more complex and more competitive. Getting a handle on what is going on in a large non-profit organization is difficult enough for a full-time manager. But for a volunteer board member, it is no longer the rule to expect to sit in a room four times a year and listen to perfunctorily recited reports from staff and "dog and pony show" PowerPoint presentations.

The board member in modern times has recognized that he or she can no longer afford to risk being the silent partner, and has the right and even the duty to seek and obtain full access to all of the information needed to permit him or her and his or her colleagues to guide the organization's future, beginning with hiring or firing the executive director, and including whether to implement a change management strategy. The board of directors, collectively and individually, must act to preserve and protect not only the organization's financial assets, but its intangible assets (such as the good name of the organization), as well.

There is a classic saying attributed to political scientist Wallace Sayre that public management and private management are the same in all unimportant respects. That goes as well for a comparison of non-profit and for-profit boards. One of the most important differences is that non-profit boards typically stick to the core mission of their organization, even if opportunities avail themselves that may be "profitable."

A second major difference is that many are driven by the exigencies of fundraising; in fact, unlike most for-profit board members who are paid, there is often an "admission fee" for serving on a non-profit board consisting of a written or unwritten requirement that a sizable charitable donation be made to the organization annually. Some foundations will even look at the degree to which board members participate in fundraising appeals as a factor in evaluating whether to make grants.

Third, non-profit boards must be accountable to many other stakeholders, such as clients, donors, political and community leaders, the media, and the public at large. For-profit companies generally are accountable only to the stockholders of the company. Non-profit boards are generally larger than their for-profit counterparts, and tend to be more pluralistic, building a political coalition to maintain wide community support for the organization. As a byproduct of this diversity, it is often more difficult to reach a consensus on making transformational changes, particularly since the predicted outcome of the change by its advocates may not be simply measured in "increased profit," but rather a less easily measurable improvement in public service provided by the non-profit organization. While for-profit board members can debate whether one strategy will increase profit or not, there is at least a common currency and value being considered.

In non-profit board debate over a change in policy, the values may conflict and be much more nebulous. It is difficult to factor in the "opportunity cost" when that cost is measured in improvement to the community and society rather than in dollars. One additional complication resulting from a diverse board is that there are likely to be more hidden agendas. It is certainly simpler when the agenda, hidden or explicit, is to increase profit. All of these factors make coming to a consensus much more difficult in a non-profit organization.

The core values of an organization are often shaped by the board. For example, looking at the type of executive director hired by the board is one major way these values are instilled. For example, has the board chosen someone with a master's in Social Work (MSW), whose education was likely shaped by humanistic concerns and serving client needs, or a master's in Business Administration (MBA), who was touted as being able to get rid of all of the dead wood and beat the competition into the ground? Does the board have difficulty approving projects utilizing new technologies? Are budgets expected to be incremental? Is the executive director given a long leash or a short leash? Does the board schedule retreats with key staff to plan strategically? Does the board hire consultants to help it solve problems and does the board take their advice or use them as window dressing? How often does the board change its own internal procedures to accommodate the needs of new members or to adjust to changing conditions? How important is quality with respect to the board's internal procedures?

Answers to these and related questions provide cues to staff on the values of the organization, and are significant in establishing a baseline for organizational culture, particularly in new organizations.

John Carver, in his landmark book *Boards That Make A Difference*, proposed a new paradigm for board-CEO relations. In simple terms, the role of the board in the Carver model is to stay out of day-to-day management and instead concentrate on setting out in broad terms what goals the CEO is expected to accomplish, and the broad constraints and rules. In this model, the board's role is to determine ends and outcomes. The board is also charged with explicitly devising general constraints on how the executive may achieve these outcomes (such as prohibiting discrimination and establishing grievance procedures for employees) that the CEO is expected to follow. Carver's influence has gone far beyond the non-profit sector, as leaders of all types of organizations have recognized the value of his new way of looking at the balance of power between those who govern organizations and those who manage them on a day-to-day basis.

**Board and Management Attitudes About Quality**

A study of the respective roles of boards and management on the issue of total quality was commissioned by the American Society for Quality Control (ASQC) and carried out by the Gallup organization in 1993. Many were surprised by the results, which showed an astounding degree of agreement between upper-level corporate executives and a smaller sample of outside directors. Participants in the survey were asked to rate on a 10-point scale whether management or the board had responsibility for determining quality policy, with "10" indicating that management had total authority and "1" that the board had total authority. Two-thirds of the managers responded with a rating of 8, 9, or 10, although service companies (presumably as would be the case in non-profit organizations) showed less of a tendency to favor total management responsibility. Two-thirds of the outside directors also gave the response an 8, 9 or 10, although only about 15% rated this a 10 compared to 35% of executives.

The survey also considered whether respondents felt this balance between board and management responsibility would be changing. The results indicated that both managers and board members felt that this balance would not be changing.

Charles A. Aubrey III, a member of the National Productivity Review Editorial Advisory Board and Chairman of ASQC, writing in *Should the Board of Directors be Involved in TQM?* (Summer, 1993 issue of *National Productivity Review*), implies that successful companies with strong board chairs recognize that they can't be silent and have a hands-off policy. Instead, they must be partners in the total quality effort.

John Nash, president of the National Association of Corporate Directors, when interviewed in the same article, said:

> *For boards, quality is an indirect issue—a management issue. Boards in the United States don't intervene unless they think there may be a problem. They want to know 'Are we competitive? If not, why is quality a factor here?' It's a management responsibility to brief the board on quality matters. Boards don't manage. Quality falls within management's purview unless the board has set a policy on quality.*

This contrasts sharply to the view of John Carver. Carver says in his book that boards should be more proactive with quality issues, and that continual improvement goes against the tradition of organizations with long histories. The conventional way that boards operate disempowers management and becomes meddlesome. There is a contradiction in simultaneously tying the hands of top management by micromanaging TQM at the board level, and the empowering of employees (including the manager)—one of the tenets of TQM. Carver suggests that the board should be talking about quality as an outcome for management to achieve and be judged by, but it should be up to management to find the means to reach those goals without interference from the board. However, it is the board's responsibility to pursue excellence in the governing process itself.

Aubrey, in the same article referred to earlier, suggests that quality cannot happen without quality commitment and involvement from the very top, without clear direction and support from the board. The board must be knowledgeable enough to provide oversight, ask the right questions, request pertinent reports, and provide management with a basis for fair accountability.

Perhaps the board's role can be that of a coach and mentor on quality. Certainly, board members come from diverse settings—many serve on other boards where TQM or another change management strategy has either been implemented or planned. Some may be CEOs themselves who have dabbled with TQM and have firsthand knowledge about its benefits and pitfalls. Boards can be a valued resource to managers planning TQM. What the board shouldn't be doing, as Carver suggests in his philosophy, is telling management which computer statistical package to implement, which mid-level manager to honcho the program, and what the recognition program should be.

One provocative finding of this survey with implications for managers instituting a TQM program is that board members were more interested in looking at reports related to customer satisfaction measures and indicators of quality already achieved, as opposed to quality plans that would set the course for the future.

One conclusion that can be drawn is that when TQM programs are contemplated by top managers, it is important to create a path for board acceptance of the TQM planning process. This can be arduous and it can take years before results show up in the reports of customer satisfaction, which are the fodder of boards. Also, the survey showed that boards are interested in comparisons with past performance of an organization, rather than comparisons with competitors or evaluations in absolute terms.

Boards can play a pivotal role in creating an environment that facilitates the adoption of change management strategies as politically transforming as TQM. It may make a big difference in the board's attitude if the suggestion to pursue TQM as an option comes from an active board member rather than from management. In either case, it is management's responsibility to educate the board about what is involved with TQM (or, for that matter, any other change management strategy), including the costs, the expected benefits, the time frame involved, the organizational resources that will be devoted to it, the personnel who will be assigned to perform the training (either outside consultants or from within the organization), the extent to which similar or competing organizations are utilizing TQM, and what objectives are to be accomplished.

In organizations whose boards think the Carver model is a simple ruse to shift power from the board to management and fail to grasp the vision inherent in Carver's new paradigm, obtaining approval to begin implementing a change management strategy may be as difficult a task for management as the actual implementation. The CEO suddenly smitten with TQM may have a vision of an agency that places the customer first, but that epiphany may have been the result of that manager's entire professional life (and, perhaps some of his personal life consisting of sleepless nights worrying about the organization's future) focusing upon the organization, its shortcomings, and its potential to achieve greatness, or, at least, remain competitive. Board members of a voluntary organization, on the other hand, may be contemplating issues relating to that organization for perhaps a total of three or four hours every three months, and they may have virtually no clue about the day-to-day costs of quality failures that may be invisible to the board, the public, and other stakeholders, but which create those sleepless nights for the CEO.

Unlike their for-profit counterparts, who often receive lucrative compensation for their board services, those who serve on non-profit organization boards do so, almost universally, as volunteers and from a sense of *noblesse oblige.* Many board members may be from professions that have minimal exposure to change management strategies, and may be totally unfamiliar with TQM, and skeptical about calls to implement it without putting up substantial resistance. CEOs need to be sensitive to the fact that boards are not likely to perfunctorily authorize TQM interventions without months, or perhaps years, of study, perhaps by an internal board committee. CEOs may find the board authorizing a cautious, toe-in-the-water, skeletal implementation of TQM that, of course, is antithetical to TQM principles almost by definition. Savvy CEOs will recognize that group decision-making is not the best environment for making decisions about change management.

To overcome this, CEOs should continually be bombarding board members with journal articles and news clippings about quality management successes well before any proposal to implement organizational TQM adoption is considered. It takes time to plant the seed of enthusiasm for TQM in a board of directors, and if the board remains unconvinced, TQM proposals may be placed on the scrap heap along with other proposals that may have not found an effective voice of advocacy within the board.

## Up Close: Dr. Channing Hillway

Dr. Channing Hillway, a non-profit organizational consultant based in Ventura, California, is a regular contributor to the soc.nonprofit.org electronic mailing list, where experts and novices alike share their problems and seek advice. He received his doctorate in leadership, policy, and complex organizations, from the University of California, Santa Barbara. He has worked with both large and small non-profit organizations. One of his current interests is Total Quality Management under the broader context of communication, and he is working on a textbook targeted to students who are hoping to become professionals in the communication areas or are seeking to enhance personal and organizational excellence.

"The non-profit sector has been less attuned to quality issues due to the nature of the people who participate," he observes. "People are drawn to work as volunteer board members and workers for their own reasons and there is a reluctance (by an organization's leadership) to directly address the intentions and competencies of such persons."

Hillway feels that those involved in non-profit organizations have different, not necessarily better or worse, motivations than those who are drawn to for-profit organizations. But generally, this difference results in large variations in the dynamics within the two types of organizations.

"The paid professionals are often working for lower salaries than their counterparts in the private sector and everyone seems to be endeavoring to avoid unnecessary conflict," he analyzes. "The big issues are how more funding can be found to carry on the work and how can everyone feel okay about being part of the team. What that really means, then, is that small non-profits tend to exhibit the same behaviors we see in public schools and bureaucracies—a reluctance to directly address personnel and efficiency problems. The myth is maintained that everything is just fine in the organization when it may not be."

Eventually, some event occurs that brings the organizational leadership back to reality, and facilitates its focus on solving problems that have either been swept under the rug or ignored as a result of organizational denial.

"A crisis provides a window of opportunity for the organization," he points out, giving an example of one non-profit client, a choral group, which was immobilized by the resignation of a key staff member.

"The organization put on several major concerts each year with full orchestra, and was partially paralyzed by the executive director's determination to maintain control over everything," Hillway relates. "She continued to ask for volunteers and then micromanaged them to death, so that people were moving in and out of committee and project positions." As a result, the pool of volunteers was dwindling while the organization was growing. "The exec claimed that the relationships she had built in the community over many years meant that only she could do certain tasks and held such tasks as her own sacred trust. When she resigned her position, there was simply no one with the time to take her place.

"A part-time exec was hired who immediately began recruiting people for various tasks, and then empowered them to do the work," he continues. "The organization has experienced an explosion of volunteerism and is healthier than it has been in years. The change took place, however, with very little effort to implement TQM or any similar plan. People were not asking the questions that would lead to a discussion of any structured form of organizational development. Instead, they just wanted to get to work, and they wanted permission to show what they could do."

He feels that board members play a key role in promoting improvement of quality and performance of non-profit organizations.

"I believe that only when there is a critical mass of leadership people—board members who understand quality management—are the right questions asked and the door opened for any significant, structured organizational development effort," he says.

As an organizational consultant, he expresses his frustration at clients who fail to recognize that their organizations can use some "therapy" with respect to quality management and improving business processes. Organizations are often eager to hire outside consultants to improve fundraising and grantsmanship, but are less likely to invest in services designed to promote organizational development. One particular client is a candidate for organizational intervention, Hillway says, although the organization hired him solely to develop grant proposals.

"The problem here is, once again, with an exec who has grown into his position in the organization—a drug and alcohol rehabilitation center whose clients include many homeless people—and has proven his value as a hands-on leader," he describes. "He is now faced with moving to a higher level of leadership and needs assistance. The assistance he wants, however, is not the assistance he needs. He needs help with restructuring the way he and his organization get things done. I have offered my services in this area and the non-verbals I received in return suggested people were alarmed at the prospect of having to begin paying for something for which they believe they have already been paying."

Hillway predicts that a crisis in this organization will occur in the near or distant future, opening the door to change. In the meantime, he says, the door to solving the problem is closed. Change management strategies, such as TQM and BPR, often provide the forum to discuss organizational problems and involve all members of the organization in seeking solutions. And that can't be a bad thing, he summarizes.

# 9
# Concluding Comments

Those reading this book are highly likely to have an identification with a non-profit organization, either as a manager or board member, and are searching for ways to make it perform better. Unfortunately, there are no magic potions or magic bullets to accomplish this, regardless of how much time and money you are willing to invest. But I can say with some confidence that organizations must change or die. There are few organizations we know of today that existed a hundred years ago. What happened to those that are no longer here? And what can you do to make yours serve the public longer than it otherwise would have? The answers to these questions are elusive.

As we enter the new millennium, the non-profit sector appears to be thriving in the United States. Despite highly publicized scandals involving some of the best-known organizations in the sector, public confidence in the ability of charities to respond to the ever burgeoning needs for human services remains high. The "halo effect," a public perception that charities are intrinsically better to do business with than their for-profit counterparts, is still intact.

Obviously, challenges lie ahead. At the global level, many economists warn of a world-wide depression, Other problems, such as the population explosion, global warming and other climate changes, natural disasters, famine, outbreaks of epidemics, armed conflicts, the destruction of fragile ecosystems, the depletion of natural resources, nuclear proliferation, terrorism, and the threatened resurgence of totalitarianism are among issues that will command our attention. Non-profit organizations, with their government partners, are on the front lines of solving, or at least mitigating, these problems. Environmental degradation, structural unemployment, racism, poverty, cancer, and homelessness are among the problems that government at the federal, state, and local levels, work with the voluntary sector to ameliorate.

Improving the efficiency and effectiveness of our non-profit organizations establishes and maintains their credibility when they speak out in the political debate on public-policy issues. Elements within the United States Congress have been skeptical about the need for charities to engage in advocacy, and constraints on lobbying activities continue to be proposed and debated. To this point, those who understand why charities need to be strong advocates on behalf of their clients and society at large have been successful in thwarting draconian measures to stifle and gag the non-profit sector.

One important field of action for the non-profit sector continues to be advocacy—government often provides the financial resources and the non-profit sector provides the muscle, creativity, energy, and elbow grease to accomplish what government, by itself, might otherwise be unable to do. The non-profit sector has expertise on virtually every public-policy issue and also serves as a public-policy conscience. I believe one way to stave off this legislative threat is for quality to pervade the consciousness of every non-profit manager, and for all legislators to be exposed in their districts to non-profit organizational programs that are exemplars. Political power of the non-profit sector can be expanded if the sector enhances its perception as a provider of quality goods and services.

Those who manage non-profits today demonstrate a high degree of professionalism, experience, intelligence, and commitment to serve the public good while often sacrificing their own material wants. To an increasing degree, non-profit managers come to the table with advanced degrees and technical management training. Colleges and universities have recognized the demand for continuing education courses and full-degree programs catering to non-profit managers and those who seek to enter the field. Many who graduate from these programs sustain an unquenchable desire for more education in order to improve their personal performance and achievement and that of their organizations.

For most of us, running a non-profit organization is not just a "job." We talk about our organization's problems at the dinner table, at the ball game, and at parties. It permeates our dreams at night. It is ingrained in our culture to focus on our work, and most of those employed by non-profit organizations are quite satisfied, if not proud, with being a part of a sector that is committed to placing human needs first rather than making a profit for stockholders. The apparently intractable global and national problems mentioned earlier in this chapter must be, and will be, on the public-policy agenda, and non-profit organizations will play a key role in developing creative solutions for them. If we can be successful in improving the general quality and performance of non-profits, then solving these problems will likely be quicker and accomplished with fewer resources.

We must make this a goal.

Some of the management strategies described in this book are designed to help in this effort. It is not just our organizations and ourselves that benefit from improved quality and performance of the organizations we manage. Our clients and the public are the ultimate beneficiaries.

**Organization Theory**

Management of organizations is part art, part craft, and part science. Organizational theorists have written volumes, and engaged in hundreds, if not thousands, of empirical studies to get to the core of how to increase organizational effectiveness. Organizational science is still in its infancy, and it may be too soon to tell, but I suspect that science will not come up with much to say that will revolutionize the way organizational leaders improve their organizations. Many established figures in the field express their frustration with how very little we know about what makes organizations tick.

Just as "art" has its schools, often reflecting the dominant social paradigms of the time (Baroque, classical, impressionist, modern, post-modern, among others) organizational theory can boast of distinct schools. Herbert Simon, in the latest edition of his classic work *Administrative Behavior*, describes some of them—classical, neoclassical, human resources, "modern" structural, systems, contingency, and population ecology.

Organizational theory encompasses a panoply of wide-ranging ideas, some of which are empirically based, and others that are highly theoretical. Among some of the best-known organization theories are the following:

**1. Organizations are like machines.**

Max Weber's writings, not published in the United States until 1947, nearly three decades after his death, were influential in providing a framework for the nature of bureaucratic hierarchies and the efficiency of decisions made rationally from the perspective of the organization rather than emanating from the personal needs of the organization's leader. Non-profit organizations differ minimally from their government or their for-profit counterparts in the extent to which they form bureaucratic hierarchies. There are principles, some of them contradictory, as Herbert Simon has pointed out, that govern grouping of bureaus (such as by function, geography, process, or clientele). Each employee has one boss to report to, with a chain of command. Work is divided by specialization. Each manager has a "span of control" restricted to 5-8 workers.

The Scientific Management approach of Frederick Taylor, which came to prominence early in the 20th century, is based on this perspective. It is still a major influence on organizations such as those in the fast-food industry. In this model, managers do the thinking and planning, and the workers do the work. Workers are not paid to think, but to follow management's prescription for doing a job, which is often described in excruciatingly explicit detail. In non-profit settings, one can find this management perspective less and less. Of course, you can find it in a sheltered workshop, and perhaps in a hospital cafeteria.

There are few non-profits that don't have a structure that is based on the bureaucratic model of organization. Non-profits of the future may adopt various alternatives. Among such alternatives are virtual organizations (where management and coordination may be performed online among workers who may not have a formal work relationship with the organization) and matrix management models (where groups form to solve problems with minimal relationship to an established organization hierarchy).

**2. Organizations are open systems.**

Daniel Katz and Robert Kahn in their 1966 book, *The Social Psychology of Organizations*, and James Thompson in *Organizations in Action*, are among the leading proponents of this descriptive theory. Its basic tenet is that organizations are open systems. This model of organization is based on the work of Ludwig von Bertalanffy, a German biologist who, along with several others working independently on several continents, developed the concepts of General Systems Theory. This theory sees organizations as dynamic systems with inputs (personnel, supplies, information), throughputs (work processes that are performed on the inputs), and outputs (the finished product, services, and information transported to the environment), which are influenced by positive and negative feedback. Under this frame of reference, the bureaucratic model of Weber described above assumes organizations are closed systems, only minimally influenced by factors emanating from outside the organization.

**3. Organizations are part of an ecology.**

A corollary to the systems approach is that organizations are similar to biological systems. They have a life cycle, grow, become more complex, seek homeostasis (a process in which their internal controls are maintained despite pressures from outside forces to upset these controls), import "energy" to combat the effects of entropy, do what is necessary to survive, and potentially enter a state of equifinality, a final state resulting from the effects of increased entropy where there is minimal change going on inside and "death" is quite possible.

This theory took hold in the 1970s, about the same time as the environmental movement in the United States, and focuses on why there are so many types of organizations. The history and research associated with this theory is described by Joel A. C. Baum in *Organizational Ecology* (*Handbook of Organization Studies*, p. 77).

**4. Organizations are crucibles of human behavior.**

This theory (supported by the work of M. P. Follet, H. Minzberg, D. McGregor, A. Maslow, R. Likert, and others) maintains that organizations consist of thinking humans who act nothing like cogs in a machine perfunctorily performing the jobs the way management tells them to do (such as would be the case in the Weberian ideal bureaucracy or Frederick Taylor's "one best way" to perform a job). Organizations consist of individuals with needs (organizational needs, personal needs, career needs, and so on), and they act to meet those needs. The informal organization may be as influential as the formal organization in affecting behavior in organizations. Human relations theory predicts that one cannot expect to obtain efficiency and effectiveness by treating people like machines, as Frederick Taylor's theory suggests, and that managers who pay attention to those needs get better results.

5. **Organizations act to maximize their utility**.

This perspective looks at individuals as acting in their own self-interest and motivated by maximizing their utility. It encompasses the theory of *Incrementalism* (Charles Lindblom, 1959). Herbert Simon's theory on decision-making asserts that managers do not make decisions "rationally" by choosing the best among all available alternatives but rather "satisfice"—choose from among a few choices, and selecting the one that is satisfactorily solving a problem. Dr. Lindblom took this theory one step further by suggesting that decisions tend to be incremental, contending that organizations act to ameliorate the worst effects of problems rather than solve them. This is because solving them is too complicated and requires too much political capital to be expended. Thus, an organization's budget often provides for an incremental increase for each program, and the Manhattan Project and the Apollo Program are anomalies in a public-policy process that seeks to generate political acceptance and consensus by not taking too many giant steps toward dealing with a problem. The market approach also includes Transaction Cost Theory, which asserts that organizations rationally choose between "making" a product or service in-house or "buying" the product or service in the marketplace. The decision is based on which has the most transaction costs, including finding a vendor, negotiating a contract, enforcing the contract, and assuring quality of the product or service when delivery by the contractor occurs.

6. **Organizations have a unique culture.**

This culture comprises values, norms, behavioral regularities, and unwritten rules which capture the organization's view of itself and its place in the environment, and affect both the organization and its task environment (defined as those outside of the organization who directly influence the ability of the organization to achieve its goals, such as suppliers, customers, and regulators). Theory suggests that organizational members must learn and accept this culture to succeed, and that the organization's culture must be consonant with its task environment.

7. **Efficiency is contingent upon conditions and circumstances.**

    This theory maintains that the most-efficient structure for an organization is determined by its goals and social and technical circumstances. This theory emphasizes the complex nature of organizations and attempts to understand which is the most-efficient structure based on varying conditions and in specific circumstances. The research conducted by Burns and Stalker, Joan Woodward, Charles Perrow, Lawrence and Lorsch, and James D. Thompson on organizational structure efficiency is consistent with contingency theory.

**The Science of Organizations**

The academic literature reflects an ambivalence about the validity and practicality of organizational theory. It purports to provide scientific answers to how large and small organizations behave. But it suffers from the delusion that it can actually do so. The reason is it often uses the same methods and frames of reference which are used to measure inanimate objects. Organizations consist of people who interact in unpredictable ways, reacting not to each other like atoms and molecules, but rather through exchanges of values, needs, experiences, goals, and randomly conveyed thoughts.

The inability for science to come up with a single, useful theory of organizations is anticipated by chaos theory (see Chapter 7). Clearly, organizations are dynamic, non-linear systems. They are sensitively dependent on initial conditions. Even under hypothetical conditions in which there are only two members of an organization, the two members are genetically identical, and the entire environment is totally controlled by the experimenter, chaos theory suggests that this organization will grow, require inputs, produce outputs, develop work processes, develop an organizational culture, develop a culture and sociotechnical system, in a manner that is different each time the experiment is conducted.

This is not to say that one can't perform experiments and make useful generalizations about organizations. But this is analogous to a baseball manager's dilemma in deciding whether to avoid a double-play by sending the runner on first with less than two out and a 1-2 count on the batter. The manager may have the benefit of a computer printout on this issue with more than 100 years of statistical data. But generally, the manager makes a decision based on too many variables that can't be factored into the statistical data, such as whether the sun is shining brightly, the confidence of the batter, the speed of the runners, the characteristics of the pitcher, and perhaps a thousand other factors, which blend into a blur of a decision based on Herbert Simon's concept of "bounded rationality" or, as is more likely to be the case, "gut reaction" rather than rationality.

Baseball, in some respects, has some of the same limitations with respect to theory as organizations. There are scientific principles to apply if one were to act scientifically and methodically capture and operationalize variables, make measurements, and analyze data. And it should be much easier to come up with scientific baseball principles than organizational principles because many of the parameters involved in baseball are defined and standardized—the ball weighs the same, the bases are always 90 feet away, the rules are immutable, the teams consist of the same players, and many other factors are controlled.

Yet baseball managers tend not to be Ph.D.s calculating every move they make on a computer. And since millions of dollars ride on whether a game is won or lost, one can assume that if Ph.D.s could do a better job of managing, then they would be running the teams rather than the Casey Stengels, Don Zimmers, and Jim Lelands, who may not have much of a formal education to boast about but are certainly good "baseball men."

For cultural reasons, the advancement of science and technology is the predominant social paradigm of Western civilization. We see it in sports, although not to as great an extent as organization theory, because the stakes are much higher in the latter. Most of us could live without baseball (after all, we have football, basketball, hockey, soccer, and lacrosse). Our entire civilization, however, is built upon, and fueled by, organizations.

It doesn't necessarily follow that science will be able to come up with hard-and-fast rules describing organizations and predicting their behavior with accuracy. As mentioned before, what we know from chaos theory suggests that will not be the case. We can, however, conduct empirical studies, and come up with theories on some aspects of organizations that will yield the same outcome when repeated. But to expect that it is only a matter of time, and a matter of will, to find the grand theory that predicts the behavior of organizations is not likely to be true.

For those of us who have spent our careers working for, working with, and even creating new organizations, this conclusion is not surprising. As I previously pointed out, we watch baseball games because even after thousands of games, we see something new and interesting each time. And the same is true for organizations, infinitely more complex dynamic systems. In organizations, the "field" changes its dimensions every day, and the "ball" gets bigger or smaller both constantly and randomly. That's one of the attributes that make them so much fun!

While organization research will fish around the edges and find a nugget of truth in empirical research, the frustration of searching for the organizational equivalent of physics' Unified Field Theory is likely to continue. This is not because researchers in organizational theory are stupid, lazy, or incompetent. If they wanted their experiments to come out clean and repeatable, they should have concentrated on linear, dynamic systems rather than non-linear, dynamic systems.

What this most likely means is that we are on our own. We cannot count on some organizational theorist with the genius of Einstein to point us to the Promised Land where every employee works hard, every client's needs can be satisfied, we are granted all of the resources we need (and at just the right time) to accomplish our objectives, every board member governs appropriately, and we never find a problem that is not solvable.

So, with all that in mind, what can a manager do to steer the organization on a course of improvement? Techniques such as TQM, BPR, benchmarking, Outcome-Based Management, and LGI are packaged ways to change an organization and make it more cognizant of the purposes for which it was formed and what it needs to do to stay competitive.

The non-profit sector is at a crossroads. The advance of technology has given non-profit organizations productivity improvement tools that only a few years ago would have been considered science fiction. And imagine the possibilities of how we will be using the Internet a few years from now!

A sector-wide commitment to improving quality has swept the manufacturing sector, and each of us has benefited as a consumer. I contend that we will benefit as well from adopting and successfully implementing a quality improvement philosophy in our non-profit organizations.

## Appendix A
## *Introduction to Statistical Process Control*

In the context of providing non-profit organization services, quality can have several meanings. The broad definition of "suitability of purpose" is of some benefit, but provides a less than satisfactory picture for typical activities performed by non-profits. Improving quality in a non-profit setting is often a matter of simple common sense. This means staff who are pleasant and professional at every point in the agency-client point of contact. It means agency communications that are accurate, easy to read, aesthetic to the eye, and invite the reader. It means meetings that start on time, have an agenda that is stuck to by the convenor, and are accompanied by meeting materials that facilitate productive interaction and participation from those who attend. And it means office space that provides a pleasant, comfortable, and functional environment for both workers and clients.

Every non-profit agency, from the one-person shop to the most complex hospital, can benefit from a philosophy that encourages continual improvement. It is rare to find a non-profit organization in which even a cursory examination wouldn't suggest improvements that are needed in physical plant, working conditions, employee morale, office policies, and business processes. Most organizations already solicit improvement suggestions, and it is not unusual to find a suggestion box accessible to both customers and staff alike where complaints and suggestions can be made anonymously. The university I attend offers a $50 reward for suggestions that not only save money but may "improve quality" as well.

Yet in many large non-profit settings, quality improvement can benefit from a more scientific, quantitative approach. Mathematically valid, statistical approaches have been developed that provide guidance to the non-profit organization manager on when action should be taken to improve quality. The philosophy and techniques of Total Quality Management (TQM) evolved from looking at variation, the deviation from a standard in a statistical way, and making rules for when adjustments should be made and when things should be left alone.

Too much variation causes problems. An organization's clients utilize services with the expectation that the service will be approximately the same each time they use it. For example, even if the services are of high quality, the consumer may complain about a perceived deterioration in service if one day the service is extraordinary in quality and the next day the service is good, but not extraordinary. That is not to say that an organization can't augment its services at special times, and engage its clients creatively. But the client must feel that if he or she is getting a service, that service will meet the client's needs in a reasonable manner, and that mistakes on the part of the organization won't result in the denial of service or service below the quality that the client has come to expect.

In a manufacturing setting, variation causes a machine to make a part that does not fall within specifications. Quality control rejects the part (and sometimes, the entire batch). The ultimate consumer of the product never knows that the machine randomly spit out a part not meeting specifications, or the person operating the machine made a mistake and produced a poor-quality part. In a non-profit setting, particularly those providing human services, the consequences of error can be life-threatening. In the case of a Meals on Wheels program, undercooking the turkey by even a few minutes can have repercussions that could threaten the lives of vulnerable clients, as well as the viability of the entire agency. Poor quality in non-profit organizations can have a steep societal cost.

The first step in improving quality is to look at each process and activity performed by the organization and concentrate on those that generate complaints, not only from agency clients but from staff and suppliers as well. What is it that the agency does, and is trying to achieve? How do the complaints relate to these? In the language of the scientist, one must *operationalize* a variable, that is, put it in terms that can be defined, measured, and tracked over time.

For example, a Meals on Wheels program wants to achieve several different objectives. It wants to make timely delivery (1) of hot (2) meals of high nutritional quality (3) and reasonable cost (4) that satisfy (5) the people receiving them. Each of these objectives can be operationalized. For example, one can make a chart for each day showing the number of meals delivered, how many meals were delivered more than an hour past the time they were supposed to be delivered (or not at all), the percentage of the meals that were delivered cold when they should have been hot, the percentage of meals that failed to meet the minimum nutrition requirements of the program, the number of meals that generated consumer complaints, and the number of meals that cost more than what was budgeted for preparing them.

There is no magic and absolute way to operationalize these variables, and much of this is as much art as science. Once the variables are operationalized, data can be collected for each. Statistically, it is very unlikely that in the course of a week, every meal will be delivered, every meal will be delivered hot, every meal will meet minimum nutrition requirements, every meal will be applauded by every client, and every meal will be prepared under budget. Despite the most careful planning, things hardly ever go as planned. According to the developers of TQM such as Deming, only about 15% of things that go wrong, i.e., 15% of failures to meet minimum standards of quality, are the fault of workers. The other 85% is attributable to problems in the system of management, and other happenstance beyond the control of the person delivering the meal. For example, there might be a flu epidemic and drivers don't report to work. An accident on the highway may delay delivery of meals. A problem with a microwave coil might result in undercooking some vegetable, generating consumer complaints.

Any number of things cause variation in the quality of a process. And it is this variation that results in poor quality. The job of the manager is to train workers to avoid the 15% of errors that they are responsible for—through continuing education, incentives to spot problems before they occur, and infusing within them a spirit of quality improvement—and to address the other 85% of errors that cause variation themselves.

The manufacturing industry developed Statistical Process Control (SPC) to provide a mathematical tool for managers to make a judgment when a process needed to be fixed, or whether variation was within acceptable limits. A process with variation within acceptable limits was called "in control" and one beyond the boundaries of acceptable limits was called "out of control." To tell whether a process is out of control and needing of attention, the average of the data for each variable being measured is calculated, and upper and lower boundaries for acceptable variability are calculated. Obviously, the low boundary for defects for any variable is zero. The upper boundary is typically taken as three times the square root of the average for each variable.

A process control chart is a graph that shows the data points over time. The acceptable boundaries (dubbed the "upper control limit," or ucl, and "lower control limit," or lcl) also appear on the graph. If any of the data points appear above (or below) the ucl or lcl, then the process is considered to be unstable and requires some adjustment. If all of the data points fall within the boundaries, then they are considered to be within acceptable statistical variation that would occur randomly. A process in control should show apparently random data points within the boundaries. Patterns, even within the boundaries, such as eight or more consecutive increases, eight or more consecutive decreases, or a cyclical nature of data points, indicate that there is something going on that should be analyzed by the manager.

New staff, trucks breaking down, or changing food suppliers, may result in finding patterns in these charts. Also, keep in mind that some of the variables may not be completely independent from each other. For example, data indicating that meals were not delivered hot may be consistent with data indicating that meals were delivered late.

There are many other mathematical tools that are used by those who engage in SPC and computer programs available commercially that process organizational data. The bibliography that begins on page 145 provides additional resources for those who want to go beyond the simple explanations and examples of SPC provided in this introductory appendix.

## Appendix B
## *Dr. W. Edwards Deming's 14 Points*

The following is excerpted from Chapter 2 of *Out of the Crisis* by Dr. W. Edwards Deming:

1. Create constancy of purpose toward improvement of product and service, with the aim to become competitive and to stay in business, and to provide jobs.
2. Adopt the new philosophy. We are in a new economic age. Western management must awaken to the challenge, must learn their responsibilities, and take on leadership for change.
3. Cease dependence on inspection to achieve quality. Eliminate the need for inspection on a mass basis by building quality into the product in the first place.
4. End the practice of awarding business on the basis of price tag. Instead, minimize total cost. Move toward a single supplier for any one item, on a long-term relationship of loyalty and trust.
5. Improve constantly and forever the system of production and service, to improve quality and productivity, and thus constantly decrease costs.
6. Institute training on the job.
7. Institute leadership (see Point 12). The aim of supervision should be to help people and machines and gadgets to do a better job. Supervision of management is in need of overhaul as well as supervision of production workers.
8. Drive out fear, so that everyone may work effectively for the company.
9. Break down barriers between departments. People in research, design, sales, and production must work as a team, to foresee problems of production and in use that may be encountered with the product or service.
10. Eliminate slogans, exhortations, and targets for the work force asking for zero defects and new levels of productivity. Such exhortations only create adversarial relationships, as the bulk of the causes of low quality and low productivity belong to the system and thus lie beyond the power of the work force.
11. a. Eliminate work standards (quotas) on the factory floor. Substitute leadership.

b. Eliminate management by objective. Eliminate management by numbers, numerical goals. Substitute leadership.

12. a. Remove barriers that rob the hourly worker of his right to pride of workmanship. The responsibility of supervisors must be changed from sheer numbers to quality.

    b. Remove barriers that rob people in management and in engineering of their right to pride of workmanship. This means, *inter alia*, abolishment of the annual merit rating and of management by objective.

13. Institute a vigorous program of education and self-improvement.

14. Put everybody in the company to work to accomplish the transformation. The transformation is everybody's job.

## Appendix C
## *The Building Blocks for Return-on-Investment: Nine Key Questions**

**1. How many clients are you serving?**

When does a client become a client? Duplicated or unduplicated count.

**2. Who are they?**

Basic demographics such as age, gender, income, employment, education, disability level, race, and ethnicity.

**3. What services do you give them?**

There can be multiple services within a single program or process. Establish the number of services delivered. (Sometimes the number of clients is used in lieu of the number of services.)

**4. What does it cost?**

Identify hidden administrative costs, personnel costs and benefits, and client income transfers. Derive the total cost of providing the services.

**5. What does it cost per service delivered?**

Divide the total cost by either the number of services delivered or the number of clients served, as appropriate.

**6. What happens to the clients as a result of the service?**

There can be multiple outcomes for each service delivered. Establish a number of successful outcomes.

**7. What does it cost per outcome?**
Divide the total cost by the total number of positive outcomes.

**8. What is the value of a successful outcome?****

Establish the financial value of each individual success.

**9. What is the return on investment?****

A. Rate of Success: Divide the total number of successful outcomes by the total number of units of service.

B. Absolute ROI:

   1. Gross ROI: Multiply the total number of successful outcomes by the $ value of a successful outcome.

   2. Net ROI: Subtract the cost of the total expenditures from the Gross ROI.

C. Ratio: Divide the Gross ROI by the cost of the total expenditures.

**Example 1: Welfare to Work****

**1. How many clients are you serving?**
Answer: 100

**2. Who are they?**
Answer: TANF (Temporary Assistance to Needy Families)

**3. What services do you give them?**
Answer: Referrals to job-readiness courses, training, jobs, and follow-up services after job placement

**4. What does it cost?**
Answer: $50,000

**5. What does it cost per service delivered?**
Answer: $50,000/100 = $500/client

**6. What happens to the clients as a result of the service?**
Answer: 10 clients obtain permanent employment

**7. What does it cost per outcome?**
Answer: $50,000/10 clients = $5,000/job/client
(This is the cost of success!)

**8. What is the value of a successful outcome?****
Answer: Save $16,000 per year per family welfare costs

**9. What is the return on the investment of $50,000?****

A. Rate of Success: $\frac{\text{10 successful clients}}{\text{100 clients served}}$ = 10% ROI

B. Absolute ROI:
1. 10 clients x $16,000 = $160,000 Gross ROI
2. $160,000 - $50,000 =$110,000 Net ROI

C. Ratio:

$\frac{\$160{,}000}{\$\ 50{,}000} = \frac{\$3.20}{\$1.00}$ Relational ROI

$1 of investment yields $3.20 of return

**Example 2: Early Intervention****

**1. How many clients are you serving?**
Answer: 100

**2. Who are they?**
Answer: Children two years of age who have been assessed, and are determined to be, eligible for early-intervention services

**3. What services do you give them?**
Answer: Speech therapy, physical therapy, development support until entry into kindergarten, for a period of three years

**4. What does it cost?**
Answer: $900,000/3-year period or $300,000/1-year period

**5. What does it cost per service(s) delivered?**
Answer: $900,000/100 = $9,000/child/3 years or $3000/child/1 year

**6. What happens to the clients as a result of the service?**
Answer: 50 children enter kindergarten with no developmental delays as indicated on standardized tests during the first month of school

**7. What does it cost per outcome?**
Answer: $900,000/50 children = $18,000/child/3 years or $6000/child/1 year

**8. What's the value of a successful outcome?****
Answer: Savings of $4,000 per year per child for special education services after entry into public school

**9. What is the return on the $900,000 investment?****

A. Rate of Success: $\frac{\text{50 successful students}}{\text{100 students}}$ = 50% ROI

B. Absolute ROI:

1. 50 students x $4,000 = $200,000 Gross ROI (year 1)
2. $200,000 - $300,000 = -($100,000) Net ROI (year 1)

C. Ratio: $\frac{\$200,000}{\$300,000} = \frac{\$0.67}{\$1.00}$ Relational ROI

First-year return is less than the investment, $1 of investment yields $0.67 of return; however, the program has a 12-year payback period.

$4,000 x 12 grades = $48,000 per child over 12 years

1. 50 x $48,000 = $2,400,000 Gross ROI (public school lifetime)

2. $2,400,000 - $900,000 = $1,500,000 Net ROI (public school lifetime)

$\frac{\$2,400,000}{\$900,000} = \frac{\$2.67}{\$1.00}$ Relational ROI (public school lifetime)

$1 of investment yields $2.67 of return

*Adapted with permission from the author, Reginald Carter.
**Adapted with permission from the authors, Frederick Richmond and Eleanor Hunnemann.

# Appendix D
## *Internet Resources*

*Note: These are some of the best sites on quality that I've found on the World Wide Web. They are current as of September 1998. Site addresses and content are subject to change. For a comprehensive book on how to connect to the Internet; use it for non-profit organization applications such as fundraising, advocacy, hiring; and find hundreds more sites of interest to non-profits, obtain* The Non-Profit Internet Handbook. *An order form for this publication can be found in the back of this book.*

## *Benchmarking*

**Best Manufacturing Practices Program (Department of the Navy's Office of Naval Research)**
http://www.bmpcoe.org

This site provides information about participating in the office's best-practices program. The program, free of charge, provides voluntary best-practice surveys and reports conducted by teams of government and industry experts on defense-related organizations. The purpose of the College Park, Maryland-based program is to "increase the quality, reliability, and maintainability of goods produced by American firms" by identifying and documenting best practices, and encouraging government, industry, and academia to share information about them. While geared to manufacturing organizations, organizations in all types of business areas are invited to participate.

**The Benchmarking Exchange**
http://www.benchnet.com

This site includes survey data about the business processes most benchmarked which, when this site was reviewed, listed the benchmarking practice itself as the number three most benchmarked business process— behind human resources (#1) and information services (#2), and just ahead of purchasing/ accounting (#4) and customer services (#5).

**The Global Procurement and Supply Chain Electronic Benchmarking Network (GEBN)**
http://gebn.bus.msu.edu

The Network is "a third-party procurement and supply chain benchmarking effort" sponsored by the Eli Broad Graduate School of Management at Michigan State University. Its primary mission is "to collect and disseminate information concerning the best procurement and supply chain strategies, practices and processes being employed by companies across industries worldwide." Its more than 200 company members worldwide "regularly provide information about their current and future competitive procurement and supply chain business practices, and management strategies," according to the site.

**Quality Network**
http://www.quality.co.uk/quality/benchadv.htm

This Web page, sponsored by the commercial, United Kingdom-based firm P. Griffin & Associates, has an excellent article introducing benchmarking practices.

**USDA Research Education Economics (REE)**
http://www.ars.usda.gov/afm/tqm/tips/bench.htm

This is an excellent introduction to benchmarking, based on a 1989 book published by ASQC Press, *Benchmarking: The Search for Industry Best Practices That Lead to Superior Performance,* by Robert Camp.

## *Business Process Reengineering*

**BPR Help Desk**
http://www.dtic.mil/bpr-helpdesk/collect.html

This page includes a bibliography of useful BPR material with hundreds of abstracts.

**BPR Online Learning Center**
http://www.prosci.com/mod1-tools.htm

Click on the link "Introduction to BPR" for a nice description of what BPR is all about. There are many other useful files at this site as well. Related change management online tutorials are also available at this site.

**Electronic College of Process Innovation**
http://www.dtic.mil/c3i/bprcd/

This site bills itself as "your knowledge center for a comprehensive set of documents, tools, and guidebooks available on the topic of business process change and creating customer value." It is sponsored by the Assistant Secretary of Defense for Command, Control, Communications and Intelligence. There are links here to university programs, associations, government resources, and quality-related media, as well as relevant electronic mailing lists.

**Holland & Davis, Inc.'s Change Management Library**
http://www.utsi.com/wbp/reengineering/faq.html

This is a commercial site for a consulting company that also markets *The Change Management Toolkit for Reengineering*, a comprehensive program for businesses contemplating reengineering efforts. One valuable feature of this site is a 10-file FAQ which includes files such as *What is reengineering?*, *Why reengineer?*, and *What's the difference between reengineering and other continuous improvement programs?* Surf to http://www.utsi.com/wbp/reengineering/resources.html for some links to other useful Internet sites.

**MIT's Tech Talk**
http://web.mit.edu/reeng/www/commit/reindex.html

This site includes full-text articles prepared by the university's PR Department dating back to 1993 on the BPR effort undertaken at the institution. The earlier articles have some excellent background information on its goals and objectives.

**Reengineering Resource Center**
http://www.reengineering.com/articles/index.htm

You can find a library of full-text BPR articles on this site. Click on "Glossary of Terms" for a link to the Electronic College of Process Innovation's glossaries of change management terms (see next entry).

**The Electronic College of Process Innovation**
http://www.dtic.mil/c3i/bprcd/mglossry.htm

This site is sponsored by the Assistant Secretary of Defense for Command, Control, Communications and Intelligence. A useful and comprehensive glossary of terms can be found here, and it is perhaps the most comprehensive and useful on the Internet.

## *Chaos Theory*

**Andrew Ho's Chaos Page**
http://www.students.uiuc.edu/~ag-ho/chaos/chaos.html

Andrew Ho is an engineering student at the University of Illinois at Champagne-Urbana. Here you can find pictures of attractors, fractals, an overview of chaos theory, and a bibliography.

**The Chaos Home Page**
http://tqd.advanced.org/3120/

This site, put together chiefly by Pittsburgh-area high school students, is one of the best chaos theory introductory Web sites on the Internet. At this site, you can find files on the history of chaos theory, view an animated, growing fractal, and learn about "real life" examples of chaos theory at work, such as a washing machine designed with chaos theory in mind, the stock market, the structure of coastlines, weather patterns, and waterwheels.

**Chaos, Institute of Physics**
http://www.aip.org/journals/chaos

This is the site for a quarterly journal on the topic published by the American Institute of Physics. It has a selection of full-text articles.

**Sci.nonlinear**
http://www.fen.bris.ac.uk/engmaths/research/nonlinear/faq.html

This is the Frequently Asked Questions (FAQ) file for the sci.nonlinear newsgroup.

**The Society for Chaos Theory in Psychology and Life Sciences**
http://www.vanderbilt.edu/AnS/psychology/cogsci/chaos/cspls.html

This site has lots of interesting chaos theory files, and this particular page is perhaps the most comprehensive list of chaos theory Internet resources on the World Wide Web. Click on "What is Chaos" and then click on "Basic Workshop" for a more mathematically rigorous treatment of chaos theory.

## General Quality/TQM Sites

**Associated Quality Consultants, Inc.'s Quality Resources Online**
http://www.quality.org/

This site claims to be the "most comprehensive collection of free Quality-related information, groups, discussion lists and resources in Cyberspace!" and it is difficult to argue otherwise about this self-assessment. In addition to hundreds of links to free information, resources can be purchased online by credit card. It is a great site to start exploring online quality-related Internet resources.

**Center for Quality and Productivity Improvement**
http://www.engr.wisc.edu/centers/cqpi/reports_info.htm

This is the University of Wisconsin at Madison's quality site. Click on "Management" for lists of quality-related publications, some of which are available free in full-text, provided you have an Acrobat reader (which can be downloaded free from www.adobe.com).

**Community Quality Electronic Network**
http://deming.eng.clemson.edu/pub/cqen/index.html

This Web site provides a network of community quality efforts that allows visitors to share their ideas on how to create and sustain effective cooperative efforts with other individuals and organizations pursuing quality. There is a generous supply of files about general quality management, and some useful links to other sites can be found here.

**The Continuous Improvement Monitor**
http://llanes.panam.edu/journal/cim1

This is a peer-reviewed international journal of quality systems in education published by the University of Texas Pan American's Department of School Administration and Supervision. When this site was reviewed, there was a full-text journal article available entitled *Total Quality Management: Can Education Afford to Ignore it?* The copyright disclaimer on the site provides that the "Continuous Improvement Monitor may be reproduced in whole or in part for non-profit use for the purposes of education, research, library reference, or stored or distributed as a public service by any networked computer."

**Directory of State Quality Awards**
http://www.apqc.org/statequa.htm

This site, maintained by The American Productivity & Quality Center (APQC), lists quality awards for each state, providing descriptions, contact information, and World Wide Web links where available.

**Eye on the Future: A model for TQM**
http://www.icon.co.za/~fjcm/

This site is the home page for an individual, Francis J. C. Martins. Click on the "TQM Topics" button and find provocative files on TQM, including the fascinating "Eye on the Future." The seven authors of this comprehensive and full-text document create a vision for adopting TQM principles.

**Government and Industry Quality Liaison Panel (GIQLP)**
http://ts.nist.gov/ts/htdocs/210/216/216.htm

The purpose of the GIQLP is to "construct a Quality Roadmap and to champion its implementation." Click on "Guidebooks," if you have an Acrobat reader, for a comprehensive technical paper on quality management. This site is not for novices.

**Howard Atkins' Webring**
http://ramat-negev.org.il/~howarda/ring.htm

At the time we reviewed it, 36 web sites relating to quality assurance were members of this webring.

**The Juran Institute's Juran Articles**
http://www.juran.com/juran/research

The Juran Institute has graciously provided access to hundreds of articles written by Joseph M. Juran on quality management. Users must register for access, but registration is free. Many of these articles have appeared in peer-reviewed journals.

**NASA Quality Page**
http://www.hq.nasa.gov/office/hqlibrary/hotpicks/mgt/quality.htm

This page is a bibliography of quality-related articles from many different journals, and is sponsored by the National Aeronautics and Space Administration.

**Philip Crosby Associates II, Inc.**
http://www.philipcrosby.com

In addition to being able to find information about Mr. Crosby's books, courses, audio and videotapes, and other educational materials supporting quality management, there are free resources as well. Mr. Crosby posts a newsletter on quality management called *The Centurion.* The most interesting aspect of this site is a chat room on quality and organizational reliability, which is moderated by a staff member of the organization for two hours on Tuesday mornings and Thursday afternoons.

**USDA Agricultural Research Quality Site**
http://www.ars.usda.gov/afm/tqm/afmq.htm

This is an excellent place to start for those beginning a TQM project. Click on "Quality Basics" for a primer on TQM, or "Quality Tips" for a gateway to many useful quality management files.

**W. Edwards Deming Pages at MIT**
http://www-caes.mit.edu/products/deming/home.html

You are greeted by a large color picture of the acknowledged founder of the TQM movement. The site includes lots of useful links, information about Dr. Deming's books and videos, descriptions of the Deming Institute, and a file on the 14 points for "Management System of Profound Knowledge."

## Large Group Intervention

**Bob Rouda's Home Page—Real Time Strategic Change**
http://www.alumni.caltech.edu/~rouda/T5_LSRTOD.html

Here you can find an article by Rouda and his colleague, Mitchell E. Kusy, Jr., titled *Managing Change With Large Scale, Real-Time Interventions*, which is an updated version of a journal article that first appeared in 1995.

**Community Quality**
*http://deming.eng.clemson.edu/pub/cqen/files/macatawa.txt*

Click on CQEN Library and find a comprehensive case study by Frank Heckman of Frank Heckman Consulting, Inc., titled *Does the Search Conference Deliver on its Promise?: A New Method for Achieving Community Excellence*, an article that first appeared in the *Journal for Quality and Participation.*

**Healthcare Forum Journal's Future Search**
http://www.well.com/user/bbear/weisbord.html#where

This site includes the article *Future Search: A Power Tool for Building Healthier Communities*. Marvin Weisbord discusses the principles of the Future Search technique and tells how to organize a Future Search conference.

**Reed Moomaugh & Associations**
http://www.improve.org/nhaarticle.html

This is the commercial site of an organizational development consulting firm. Here you can find the document, *Head Start of San Diego: A Case Study,* which is about a Real Time Strategic Change intervention with the Head Start agency of San Diego. The article also summarizes six principles relating to this change management strategy.

**OD Corp.**
http://www.tmn.com/~roland/what.htm

OD Corp. is a private consulting practice specializing in Large Group Interventions, which they call "Whole System Transformation." There is plenty of material explaining the services the firm provides and the techniques its staff use. Click on "Resources" for plenty of informative files that can be viewed or downloaded. Click on "links" for a comprehensive list of Web sites on both LGI and change management in general.

## *Outcome-Based Management*

**American Evaluation Association**
http://www.eval.org

While this site does not have much specifically on the outcome-based approach, it has files (click on "Documents") that provide you with a perspective on what evaluators are looking for, and the constraints they operate under, when evaluating a program.

**Performance Measurement Resources**
http://www.zigonperf.com

This site is sponsored by Zigon Performance Group, which "specializes in performance appraisal, performance management, and performance measurement systems for teams and hard-to-measure employees." Click on the "Measurement Resources" link for access to free files of sample performance measures, articles, and a comprehensive bibliography.

**United Way of America's Resource Network on Outcomes Measurement**
http://www.unitedway.org/outcomes/

Click on "Resource Network on Outcome Management" for an abridged version of the United Way publication, *Measuring Program Outcomes Training Kit.* You can find information about, and generous excerpts of, *Measuring Program Outcomes: A Practical Approach.* There are also links to organizations and publishers at this site (click on "General Education Resources"). You can also find two full-text articles on this site, *Outcome Measurement: Showing Results in the Nonprofit Sector* (http://www.unitedway.org/outcomes/ndpaper.html) and *The Status of Research and Indicators On Nonprofit Performance In Human Services* (http://www.unitedway.org/outcomes/ispaper.html).

# Bibliography

## Chapter 1— Introduction to Change Management

Grobman, Gary. (1997). *The Non-Profit Handbook, National Edition.* Harrisburg, PA: White Hat Communications.

Martin, Lawrence. (1993). *TQM in Human Service Organizations.* San Francisco: Jossey-Bass.

## Chapter 2— Introduction to Total Quality Management

Caudron, Shari. (1993). *Just Exactly What is Total Quality Management? Personnel Journal.* v72 n2. Feb. 1993. p. 32.

Costin, Harry. (1994). *Readings in Total Quality Management.* Orlando, FL: Harcourt Brace & Co.

Covey, Stephen R. (1992). *Principles of Total Quality. Modern Office Technology.* v37 n2. Feb. 1992. p. 10.

Creech, Bill. (1994). *The Five Pillars of TQM: How to Make Total Quality Management Work for You.* New York: Penguin Books.

Crosby, Philip B. (1979). *Quality is Free.* New York: McGraw Hill.

Deming, W. Edward. (1975). *On Some Statistical Aids Toward Economic Production. Interfaces,* v5, n4. Aug. 1975. The Operations Research Society of America and the Institute of Management Sciences.

Garvin, David A. (1988). *Management Quality: The Strategic and Competitive Edge.* New York: Free Press.

Geber, Beverly. (1992). *Can TQM Cure Health Care?* Training. v29 n8. Aug. 1992. pp. 25-34.

Hakes, Chris. (Editor). (1991). *Total Quality Management: The Key to Business Improvement.* London: Chapman & Hall.

Juran, J. M. (1986). *The Quality Trilogy: A Universal Approach to Managing for Quality. Quality Progress,* Aug. 1986 (excerpted in *Readings in Total Quality Management,* Harry Costin.)

Martin, Lawrence. (1993). *TQM in Human Service Organizations*. San Francisco: Jossey-Bass.

Sashkin, Marshall. (1992). *What Is TQM? Executive Excellence*. v9 n5. May 1992. p. 11.

Saylor, James H. (1996). *TQM Simplified, A Practical Guide. (Second Edition)*. New York: McGraw-Hill.

**Chapter 3—Introduction to Business Process Reengineering**

Classe, Allison. (1993). *Don't Tinker With It: BPR It!* Accountancy. v112 n1199, July 1993, pp. 64-66.

Davenport, Thomas H. (1993). *Process Innovation—Reengineering Work Through Information Technology*. Boston: Harvard Business School Press.

Hammer, Michael. (1990). *Reengineering Work: Don't Automate: Obliterate. Harvard Business Review*, July-Aug. 1990, pp. 104-112.

Hammer, Michael. and Champy, James. (1993). *Reengineering the Corporation: A Manifesto for Business*. New York: HarperBusiness.

Hammer, Michael and Stanton, Steven A. (1994). *The Reengineering Revolution: A Handbook*. New York: HarperBusiness.

Jackson, David. (1994). *BPR: Hype or Reality? TQM Magazine*. v6 n6, pp. 19-22.

MacDonald, John. (1995). *Together BPR and TQM Are Winners. TQM Magazine*. v7 n3. pp. 21-25.

**Chapter 4—Introduction to Benchmarking and Best Practices**

Bogan, Christopher E. and English, Michael. *Benchmarking for Best Practices: Winning Through Innovative Adaptation*. New York: McGraw-Hill.

Camp, Robert C. (1989). *Benchmarking: The Search for Industry Best Practices that Lead to Superior Performance*. Milwaukee, Wisconsin: ASQC Press.

Harrington, H. James. (1996). *High Performance Benchmarking—20 Steps to Success.* New York: McGraw-Hill.

Keehley, Patricia; Medlin, Steven; MacBride, Sue; and Longmire, Laura. (1997). *Benchmarking for Best Practices in the Public Sector.* San Francisco: Jossey-Bass.

Peters, Thomas J. and Waterman, Jr., Robert H. (1982). *In Search of Excellence: Lessons from America's Best-Run Companies.* New York: Harper and Row.

Steckel, Richard and Lehman, Jennifer. (1997). *In Search of America's Best Non-Profits.* San Francisco: Jossey-Bass.

Watson, Gregory H. (1992). *The Benchmarking Workbook: Adapting Best Practices for Performance Improvement.* Portland, OR: Productivity Press.

**Chapter 5—Introduction to Outcome-Based Management**

Carter, Reginald. (1983). *The Accountable Agency.* Thousand Oaks, CA: Sage Publications.

Friedman, Mark. (1997). *A Guide to Developing and Using Performance Measures in Results-Based Budgeting.* Washington, D.C.: The Finance Project.

Greenway, Martha Taylor. (1996). *The Status of Research and Indicators On Nonprofit Performance In Human Services.* Alexandria, VA: United Way of America.

Hatry, Harry; van Houton, T.; Plantz, Margaret C; and Greenway, M. J. (1996). *Measuring Program Outcomes: A Practical Approach.* Alexandria, VA: United Way of America.

Millar, Kenneth; Hatry, Harry; et al. (1981). *Developing Client Outcome Monitoring Systems.* Washington, D.C.: The Urban Institute.

Plantz, Margaret, Taylor Greenway, Martha, and Hendricks, Michael. (1997). *Outcome Measurement: Showing Results in the Nonprofit Sector: A Guide for State and Local Social Service Agencies. New Directions for Evaluation: Using Performance Measure-*

*ment to Improve Public and Nonprofit Programs* (n75, Fall 1997). San Francisco: Jossey-Bass.

Richmond, Frederick and Hunnemann, Eleanor. (1996). *What Every Board Member Needs to Know About Outcomes.* (Management and Technical Assistance Publication Series n2, Harrisburg, PA: Positive Outcomes.

**Chapter 6—Introduction to Large Group Intervention**

Bunker, Barbara Benedict and Alban, Billie T. (1997). *Large Group Interventions: Engaging the Whole System for Rapid Change.* San Francisco: Jossey-Bass.

Bunker, Barbara Benedict and Alban, Billie T. *(1992). What Makes Large Group Interventions Effective?* Journal of Applied Behavioral Science 28(4).

Coghlan, David. (1998). *The Process of Change Through Interlevel Dynamics in a Large-Group Intervention for a Religious Organization. Journal of Applied Behavioral Science.* v34 n1. March 1998. pp. 105-119.

Rouda, R. & Kusy, M., Jr. (1995). *Organization Development—The Management of Change. Tappi Journal* 78(8): 253 (1995).

Weisbord, Marvin R. & Janoff, S. (1995). *Future Search — An Action Guide to Finding Common Ground in Organizations & Communities.* San Francisco: Berrett-Koehler Publishers.

Weisbord, Marvin R. (1988). *For More Productive Workplaces. Journal of Management Consulting.* v4 n2. pp. 7-14.

**Chapter 7—Introduction to Chaos Theory**

Kiel, L. Douglas. (1994). *Managing Chaos and Complexity in Government.* San Francisco: Jossey-Bass.

Gleick, James. (1987). *Chaos: Making a New Science.* New York: Viking Penguin.

Ross, Mike, Traeger, Mike and Kraynak, Andrea. (1997). *The History of Chaos.* The Chaos Experience Internet site. (http://hyperion.advanced.org/3120).

## Chapter 8—The Role of Boards in Change Management

Aubrey, Charles A. III. (1993). *Should the Board of Directors Be Involved in TQM? National Productivity Review*. v12 n3. Summer 1993. p. 317-323.

Carver, John. (1990). *Boards That Make A Difference*. San Francisco: Jossey-Bass Publishers.

## Chapter 9—Closing Comments

Clegg, Stewart R.; Hardy, Cynthia; and Nord, Walter R. (eds.). (1996). *Handbook of Organizational Studies*. Thousand Oaks, CA: Sage Publications.

Denhardt, Robert B. (1998). *Five Great Issues in Organization Theory* (from *The Handbook of Public Administration*, Second Edition, Rabin, Jack; et al.).

Gerth, H. H. and Mills, C. Wright. (1946). *From Max Weber: Essays in Sociology*. New York: Oxford University Press.

Golembiewski, Robert. (1998). *Trends in the Development of the Organizational Sciences* (from Rabin, Jack; et al., *The Handbook of Public Administration*, Chapter 3, pp. 103-116).

Harmon, Michael M. and Mayer, Richard T. (1986*). Organization Theory for Public Administration*. Burke, VA: Chatalaine Press.

Katz, Daniel and Kahn, Robert L. (1966). *The Social Psychology of Organizations*. New York: Wiley and Sons.

Rabin, Jack; Hildreth, W. Bartley; and Miller, Gerald J. (eds.) (1998). *Handbook of Public Administration* (2nd Edition). New York: Marcel Dekker, Inc.

Simon, Herbert. (1997). *Administrative Behavior (4th Edition)*. New York: The Free Press.

von Bertalanffy. Ludwig. (1968). *General Systems Theory*. New York: George Braziller, Inc.

## About the Author

**Gary M. Grobman** received his M.P.A. from Harvard University's Kennedy School of Government and his B.S. from Drexel University's College of Science. He is in a Ph.D. program in Public Administration at The Penn State University. He currently is the special projects director for White Hat Communications and the contributing editor for *Pennsylvania Nonprofit Report.* Prior to becoming a private consultant to government, non-profit, and business organizations, he served for 13 years as executive director of the Pennsylvania Jewish Coalition, a Harrisburg-based government affairs organization representing 11 Jewish federations and their agencies. He served almost five years in Washington, D.C. as a senior legislative assistant for two members of Congress, and was a reporter and political humor columnist for the Capitol Hill independent newspaper, *Roll Call.* In 1987, he founded the Non-Profit Advocacy Network (NPAN), which consists of more than 50 statewide associations representing Pennsylvania charities. He is the author of *The Non-Profit Handbook, National Edition; The Pennsylvania Non-Profit Handbook; The Holocaust—A Guide for Pennsylvania Teachers;* and the co-author of *The Non-Profit Internet Handbook.*

## About the Contributors

**Jason Saul** is an associate in the Government Practice Group at Mayer, Brown & Platt, in Chicago, Illinois. He is also the co-founder and president of the Center for What Works, a New York-based non-profit organization that promotes benchmarking in the public sector and identifies best practices in social programming. Saul holds a Bachelor of Arts in Government and French Literature from Cornell University, a Masters in Public Policy from Harvard University's Kennedy School of Government, and a Juris Doctorate from the University of Virginia School of Law. He is also a 1989 Harry S. Truman Scholar. Saul is the author of the *Benchmarking Workbook for Nonprofit Organizations*, and has recently spoken widely on improving the effectiveness of the social sector. He was recently profiled as one of the ten social entrepreneurs in an article entitled "Young Samaritans" in *Swing Magazine.* Saul also serves on the board of the New Group at Chicago's Museum of Contemporary Art and on the Chicago Advisory Board of the International House of Blues Foundation. He can be reached at c/o MBP, 190 S. LaSalle, Chicago IL 60603. Tel: 312-701-8588; e-mail: jsaul@whatworks.org.

**Gerald Gorelick** is the President and founder of Gerald Gorelick & Associates, Inc. The firm provides organizational consulting services to small and mid-sized businesses, not-for-profit organizations, and governmental units. Large Group Interventions are the main focus of his practice. He started up the company in 1998 after 21 years of senior management experience in HMOs and insurers, hospital and health centers, and a data processing/service company, evenly split between for- and not-for-profit and ranging in size from several million to three-quarters of a billion dollars in annual revenues. He received his Bachelor's degree with distinction from the University of Michigan in mathematics and religious studies. He earned an MBA from the Wharton School of the University of Pennsylvania and an MS in computer science from the University of Toronto. His office is located at 3417 N. 4th Street, Harrisburg, PA 17110, Tel: (717)-221-1085; fax: (717) 236-0146; e-mail: Gorelev@aol.com.

**Frederick Richmond** is the founder of the Harrisburg, PA-based Center for Applied Management Practices. Founded in January 1998, the Center provides training, on-site technical assistance, MIS development and systems support, and planning assistance to non-profit organizations and agencies of local and state government. A specialty of the Center is to develop outcome-based management systems and assist agencies in preparing for managed care. Mr. Richmond has over 20 years of experience in the public-policy field, having held management positions in both federal and state government and the non-profit sector. He has served as an adjunct professor at The Pennsylvania State University. In February 1996, he co-founded the Positive Outcomes™ partnership that assisted not-for-profit and governmental entities, as well as private funding sources, in making the transition to results-oriented management and accountability. The Center is located at 222 Pine Street, Suite 300, Harrisburg, PA 17101. Tel: (717)238-7667; fax:(717)238-7699; e-mail: fkrichmond@aol.com.

## KEY WORD INDEX

### A



### *B*



### *C*



### *D*

***N***



***O***



***P***



***Q***



***R***

***Also published by White Hat Communications...***
***The Non-Profit Handbook, National Edition***
***by Gary M. Grobman***

***The Non-Profit Handbook*** is the most up-to-date and useful publication for those starting a non-profit or for those already operating one. This 302-page, 25-chapter ***Handbook*** is based on *The Pennsylvania Non-Profit Handbook,* a book originally published in 1992 with the help of more than two dozen non-profit executives and attorneys and now in its 4th edition. Each easy-to-read chapter includes a synopsis, useful tips, and resources to obtain more information. Pre-addressed postcards are included to obtain important government forms, instruction booklets, and informational publications. This essential reference tool includes:

- Information about current laws, court decisions, and regulations that apply to non-profits—two full pages devoted to each state and the District of Columbia
- Practical advice on running a non-profit, including chapters on communications, fund-raising, lobbying, personnel, fiscal management, non-profit ethics, and 19 other chapters
- Information on applying successfully for federal and state tax-exempt status
- How to write effective grant applications
- How to hire and fire
- Internet resources for non-profits
- How to develop a strategic plan
- Recent developments affecting non-profits.

We know you will find *The Non-Profit Handbook* to be an essential resource for every non-profit executive.

ISBN 0-9653653-7-9 8½" x 11" softcover 302 pages plus index

*"From the very first edition, Grobman's handbook has been a treasure. I have passed along copies to those with no knowledge of non-profit organizations as well as those with lots of hands-on experience. Its usefulness lies in its practicality and accessibility...a great resource to have on your bookshelf!"*

***—Pam Leland, Ph.D. Assistant Professor,***
***Seton Hall University***

**See order form in back of book.**

## *Also from White Hat Communications...*

***The Non-Profit Internet Handbook***
***by Gary M. Grobman and Gary B. Grant***

***The Non-Profit*** INTERNET ***Handbook*** is the definitive handbook for non-profit organizations that want to get the most out of the Internet. This is a valuable resource for:

- Non-profit organization executive staff
- Non-profit organization board members
- Those who fund non-profit organizations
- Those who contribute time and money to non-profit organizations.

*The Non-Profit* INTERNET *Handbook* includes:

- How to connect to the Internet
- How to do effective fund-raising and advocacy on the Internet
- How to develop your organization's World Wide Web site
- How to find information useful to non-profits on the Internet
- How to locate on-line sources of government, foundation, and private corporation grants.

**Plus—**
Reviews of more than 250 of the most valuable Internet sites for non-profit organizations!

This book is illustrated with Internet-related cartoons drawn by the internationally acclaimed cartoonist Randy Glasbergen, creator of *The Better Half.*

*The Non-Profit* INTERNET *Handbook* is an essential reference publication for every non-profit executive's bookshelf.
ISBN 0-9653653-6-0 8½" x 11" softcover 216 pages+index

*If you want to understand the Internet, with all that it has to offer—if you want to know exactly how the Internet can be useful to your non-profit, how it can increase your interaction with your constituency and serve to spread the word about your organization—if you need to learn to search the Web for reliable, up-to-date information on what is happening in the non-profit world, and the world in general—*The Non-Profit Internet Handbook *is the perfect gateway to the Internet galaxy."*

***—Sara E. Mélendez, President, Independent Sector***

## ORDER FORM—White Hat Communications

**Name** ______________________________

**Organization** ______________________________

**Address** ______________________________

**City, State, Zip** ______________________________

**Telephone Number** ______________________________

**Credit Card Orders:**

**Please charge:** ❑Mastercard ❑Visa

Expiration Date ______________________________

Card Number ______________________________

Cardholder's Name (Print) ______________________________

Cardholder's Signature ______________________________

**# of *Non-Profit Handbooks* Ordered____ @$29.95 ea $______**

**# of *Non-Profit Internet Handbooks* Ordered ____@ $29.95 each $______**

**# of *Improving Quality and Performance in Your Non-Profit Organization* Ordered____ @$16.95 each $______**

**Shipping and Handling ($3 per book) $______**

**TOTAL ENCLOSED $______**

**Pre-payment must accompany all orders. Please allow three weeks for delivery. Most orders are shipped priority mail.**

*For information about rush orders or quantity discounts, call (717) 238-3787. Make check or money order payable to: White Hat Communications. Pennsylvania orders: Enclose copy of PA Department of Revenue exemption certificate if claiming sales tax exemption.*

Mail to: **White Hat Communications**
**PO Box 5390**
**Harrisburg, PA 17110-0390**

**telephone/fax: 717-238-3787**

**web site: http://www.socialworker.com/nonprofit/nphome.htm**

## Other Titles Available From White Hat Communications

*The Pennsylvania Non-Profit Handbook* (4th Ed.) (1997)
*The Non-Profit Handbook, National Edition* (1997)
*The Non-Profit Internet Handbook* (1998)
*Days in the Lives of Social Workers* (1996)
*The Social Worker's Internet Handbook* (1998)
*Guide to Selecting and Applying to Master of Social Work Programs* (1999)